WHEN MONEY GET PERSONAL—
A Weekly Study

Handling Financial Dilemmas in Life's Defining Moments

BY

DAVID G. TOUSSAINT

ENDORSEMENTS

"I have known David for 25 years. He has consistently demonstrated a sincere interest in learning, teaching, and coaching finances in God's way. I encouraged him to author the book titled **'When Money Gets Personal.'** When you read it, you will be encouraged by the stories and discover wisdom and insight about handling money in God's way. This will assist you in your financial life and in your walk with Christ."

Howard Dayton, Founder, Former CEO, Compass— Well Versed In Finances

"For many years, David Toussaint has provided godly counsel to others who want to handle money wisely. Anyone looking for Bible-based, practical advice about how to be 'trustworthy in handling worldly wealth' (Luke 16:11) will benefit from reading this book."

Dr. David Faust, Associate Minister, East 91st Street Christian Church, Indianapolis, Indiana

"For nearly 20 years, David Toussaint has helped lead hundreds of people in our congregation to financial freedom. Money is central to almost everything in our lives. It addresses our security, our standing, our relationships, our children, our homes, our careers and even our future. Ecclesiastes 10:19 says, 'Money answers everything.' In this book, David clearly explains the Bible's timeless wisdom on how to be truly successful. The stories are very engaging, and the wisdom is excellent."

Dr. Darryn Scheske, Senior Pastor, Heartland Church, Indianapolis, Indiana

When my good friend David Toussaint shared with me that he was prompted to write this book, I knew that he would put his heart, mind, and passion into it. His experience and reputation as a financial coach stands firm. The real-life stories in this book will help you develop a plan for financial freedom.

David F. Altman, Pastor, Clarksville Christian Church, IN., and former President of Zimbabwe Christian College, Africa.

"The Bible tells us that God has created each of us with a tether or connection between money and possessions and our heart. The way you and I manage money and navigate the way our use of it can shape our hearts is of utmost importance.

David shares his personal testimony of coming alongside men and women through many of life's challenges. God's Word reveals principles of how we are to live, and we can find application for any financial circumstance we find ourselves in. I enjoy his posture of inquiry when encountering very difficult situations. Often asking the right next question can help people along their discipleship journey through biblical financial wisdom."

Shane Whybrew, VP of Operations for the Financial Wisdom Network, Ron Blue Institute.

CONTENTS

Introduction

1	'Breaking Up With Broke'	10
2	Taming Your Financial Excesses	39
3	Need vs Want: The Ultimate Showdown	58
4	This Is Not Working!	78
5	The Hard Path To Financial Freedom	91
6	Ensuring Long-Term Financial Stability, The Unvarnished Truth	116
7	A Life That Matters: Choices and Rewards	124
	Resource Section	144
	Index	155
	Acknowledgments	158

Note 1: Scriptures are from the New American Standard Bible (NASB) unless otherwise noted.

Note 2: **All stories in this book are real. They happened.** However, identities, locations and other aspects are changed to protect privacy.

INTRODUCTION

What qualifies me to write this book? Great question. When our church announced in 1982 that it was beginning a 'Financial Education' ministry, I thought, "This is different. You know, I will have to go to this meeting." I did and immediately joined. When I learned things like God, for real, owned everything, including all 'my' money, this meant my thinking needed to change 180 degrees. If it is all God's money, then every spending decision is a spiritual one. Whoa, every spending decision is a spiritual one? Yes, and it all comes from the Bible.

In Luke 16:11, God says, *"If therefore you have not been faithful in the use of worldly mammon (money), who will entrust the true riches to you?"* Because of this verse and others like it, I realized God related the faithfulness of my use of worldly wealth (money) to the closeness of my walk with Him. Wow! Since I wanted a close walk with Him, this meant I needed to be faithful with the money. What a concept! What a new way of thinking! This also meant I had a lot to learn. It all made great sense as I studied materials from the Christian Financial

Concepts ministry headed by Larry Burkett. I just never knew these concepts.

Years later, a friend in the ministry said, "Dave, you have got to get involved in Crown Ministries. It is a new financial ministry." I said, "What is special about Crown?" He said, "Howard Dayton is what is special. He has studied 2,350 Bible verses about money and written a powerful small group study including them. You will love it."

I did love it. In 1995, when I led my first study, I was so impressed that I began leading it multiple times. I have led it, or an updated version, over 50 times as of this writing. In addition, I received training from two of the finest financial stewardship ministers in North America, Larry Burkett and Howard Dayton.

Because Howard Dayton wrote a 'how to coach' class, I took it, too. Then, I began coaching and leading classes and eventually taught coaching.

Seeing how easy it was for Christians to mess up their finances was amazing. Why? Why was/is it so easy for Christians to mess them up? **Because they managed their finances the world's way instead of God's. God has a specific, much better plan than the world, but unless you and I know what it is, we will automatically manage our finances the world's way and find ourselves in all kinds of trouble.**

In 1998, a series of events led me to feel specifically called to this ministry. God opened a door, my wife approved, and I entered it full-time. This included leading more classes, training leaders, and, of course, more coaching.

Over the last twenty years, I encountered more stories as coaching continued. Since everyone likes stories, it occurred to me that these stories might assist others in similar situations. How could I best present this to the Christian community? It was suggested that I author this book.

It has been a difficult but rewarding effort. I am blessed that God has allowed me to participate in His ministry, blessed He has given me wisdom regarding it, and blessed I have this privilege of sharing it. I pray it will benefit you, the reader, as much as it has blessed me to live and write it. Thank you for reading.

Week 1: 'Breaking Up With Broke'

What to Do When We Have Borrowed Too Much

On April 3, 2008, I was to attend a meeting in Gainesville, Georgia. As district director for a Christian financial ministry, * I was responsible for most of a five-state area. One of the benefits of the position was an airplane I needed (wanted) to cover the area and not have to spend nights away from my young family. I was blessed to have a Beech Sierra, a plane perfect for the job.

In preparation for this trip from central Indiana, air traffic control informed me of a gigantic storm system extending from southern Indiana into north Georgia. Air Traffic Control (A.T.C.) said the only way to reach my destination by air was to go south to Memphis and

*For 13 years, I was on Crown Ministries' field staff, which became Crown Financial Ministries. In 2012, ministry changes made me part of the field staff of Compass—finances God's Way.

then east to Gainesville. I was reluctant to take this large detour, but what other options were there? The good news was that the flight to Gainesville typically took less than three and a half hours; with six hours of fuel on board, there should be plenty of fuel. When I arrived at various destinations, people typically asked me how my flight was. My answer almost always was "uneventful." Every pilot wanted this, and this flight was progressing normally.

As I approached Georgia, however, my fuel was running low – it had been a long flight, and the winds against me were more substantial than anticipated. Below me was an airport where I could land to refuel, but that would delay my already long flight even more. Not wanting to risk missing the meeting, I made the unwise choice to push forward.

I ran fuel calculations in my head, deciding I had enough to make the Gainesville airport with some to spare. Of course, there are specific rules about how much fuel reserve is required for safe operation. I would be cutting into the reserve, but there should still be some fuel left after landing.

When I arrived over the Gainesville airport, I was directed to circle around it so I could approach from the east and descend through the clouds when my instruments gave the signal. But my instruments did not give the signal. I reported this to A.T.C., and they told me to come around again for another try. I followed their directions, but again, my instruments did not give the signal to begin the descent.

At this point, A.T.C. directed me south to another airport with only scattered clouds (allowing visual flight rules rather than instrument flight rules). But that would take more fuel, fuel I now didn't have. Desperate to see the airport through the clouds below me, I would get an occasional glimpse of the ground. I saw nothing but houses and retail buildings everywhere. Did I want to try to land on one of those tiny streets with parked cars and moving traffic?

Suddenly, the engine coughed and quit. I was OUT of gas. I quickly declared an emergency to A.T.C. They connected me to another person. It dawned on me that I could switch to the fuel tank in the other wing. I flipped the switch, and the engine immediately came to life. I nearly laughed out loud with relief. But then I saw the gauge for that tank; it also showed empty.

"Do you want to cancel the emergency?" the controller asked.

"No, I need to get down quickly," I said.

"Turn to a heading of 290 degrees and descend to 1500 feet," the controller said.

I turned and began descending through the clouds. Within five minutes, I thought I had caught a runway glimpse.

"Please, let it be!" I prayed.

It was. After safely landing, I refueled the plane. Calculating the amount to refuel completely, I realized I had landed with only about six minutes of fuel left in the tank.

Was this a close call? Yes. Was I thankful I could declare an emergency with air traffic control and receive one-on-one radar direction to save my life and potentially others on the ground? Yes. Was it necessary? No. Did I learn from this? Yes, many things.

I made an <u>unwise decision</u> when I did not stop to refuel. What unwise decisions do people make today? What makes their life difficult, filling them with feelings of uncertainty?

One of the most common causes of difficulty in life is <u>borrowing, which often causes stress</u>. But there is great news, hope, and a plan. Not only is there a plan, but it is a PROVEN plan found in the Bible, the Word of Almighty God. This plan provides more than hope for your life; it provides direction and peace beyond understanding.

Please join me on a journey through the lives of many individuals and families. As they share their predicaments, we will discuss what went wrong and the steps they have taken and or can take to make it right. **We will also reveal how to <u>find the peace in life</u> we all want.**

What to do about Borrowing and Debt?
What do we do when life gets in the way? When children come unexpectedly when vehicles break down at inappropriate times when borrowing seems the only solution?

As noted, all story illustrations in this book were based on real life. Only names, locations, and personally identifying details are changed.

Life Lesson #1. Marcie and the high-interest car loan.

Marcie is married, has two children at home and one in college, and is about to graduate with her own college degree. She has been unemployed for more than a year, and with a husband who works but is partially disabled from an accident, their finances are a mess, and so are their credit scores.

In 2017, Marcie came to me for financial coaching. "We are drowning in debt. Is it possible to wipe it out somehow?"

Before I could respond, she continued. "We also need to figure out how to handle payments on a van we bought. It's five years old and seemed like a good deal for $13,000. The salesman arranged a temporary loan that we could refinance later at a lower rate. He said our payment then would be only about $170 per month. But when we sat with the banker, he apologized and said our payment would be $310. We're stuck. We had to have a reliable vehicle, but we couldn't possibly make that kind of payment. And with all our other debts, we need help. What can we do?"

Marcie and her husband are doing their best to be good Christians. But they are in a real fix with job problems, college costs, and everything else. What can they do to work their way out of this? Can we, using God's Word, help them?

Marcie and her husband have serious issues. Let's examine this more closely. She knew they had low credit scores but may not have understood the implications. Sometimes, people think they might qualify for a low rate because they *need* a low rate. Unfortunately, it doesn't work that way. She should have expected a high interest rate because of the greater risk for the lender.

It's not surprising that the salesman would suggest a payment of around $170 to entice them into the sale: that's how he makes his living. Someone with a credit score of 750 might get that rate, but not Marcie and her husband.

Unfortunately, Marcie wanted the van so much that she was not thinking straight. She allowed her emotions to carry the day when the salesman said their payment would be only about $170.

Marcie needed some wise counsel. Ideally, she would have obtained it *before* she visited a car dealer. Then, armed with proper information, she could have made a wise decision.

Regarding the choice of vehicle, good counsel in 2017 would have encouraged them to find something reliable for $6,000., less than half the price of the one they chose. It might not have looked as good, but they could not afford to drive something that looked new.

Moving to a second issue, what about the debt she wants to wipe out? It's an appealing thought – who wouldn't want that? I sure would. But a wise perspective on the matter made me realize that if I don't honor my commitments, it means:

1) I lied to the card companies when I said I would pay my bills,

2) This will 'tank' my credit score which could affect other issues such as car insurance, future auto loans, a mortgage, tenant screening, interest rates, and credit limits.

For example, when I use a credit card to buy something and do not pay, that is the same as taking the goods and not paying, which is the same as stealing. So,

Marcie is in a bind. She cannot make these payments. What should she do?

Action Step: Marcie needs a reliable vehicle but cannot afford the one she just purchased. If she and her husband truly cannot afford it, they need to sell it (even at a loss) and get one at half the cost and half the monthly payment.

Second, if the remaining debt is credit card debt, certain companies can help significantly (see below and the **specific recommendations on page 144).**

The most effective method debt management companies use is to lower credit card interest rates to 9.9%, 7.9%, or even 0%. This is how it typically works: The company charges $50 to set up your account. Next, they negotiate with the card companies to lower the rates; then they consolidate the payments into one payment, which you make each month electronically. There will be a monthly charge, which will range from $10 to $50, but because **your overall interest rate is now much lower, your total payment can be much smaller than the total of your payments before**.

Another credit card option, if you are not behind in your payments, is the debt snowball method. This is also discussed in detail on page 144. Focusing on the smallest debt and adding what you can to that debt will pay off your cards faster.

If the creditor is a company other than a credit card company, the best solution will be to contact each creditor individually. Explain your problem and promise them a certain (conservative) amount each month (be sure not to overpromise). Typically, it is better to put it in writing with a signed copy of your budget/spending plan.

If they want more information, such as who else you owe, supply this as well. This is not the time to hide anything. Your signed statement carries more weight than a verbal promise. Even if they say the amount is too small, do it anyway. If 'push comes to shove,' your proof of them accepting your partial payments will show your sincere intent to pay.

A 'last ditch' option is bankruptcy. Bankruptcy is not acceptable from God's point of view and not desirable because of the continuing ramifications it can have for up to 10 years. However, there is a type of bankruptcy that allows for additional options, such as lowering the interest rates even more than allowed by the companies on page 144 but leaves the obligation to pay the debt principal fully. See Life Lesson #7 for more details.

However, if Marcie can follow one of the plans noted above, in time, with her new degree and a good job, she and her husband will eventually pay off their debts, improving their credit scores and the outlook for their future. **The point is, "We should be proactive and run TO a solution/creditor, not away from it."**

As an aside, one man recently said he was late on his car payment. He took the advice in this book to run TO a solution (his creditors). They were so thankful he took the initiative to contact them that they said that as this was his first time being late and he had come to them, they would not show it late and even forgo the late payment penalty. What great confirmation of this advice.

There is one other point. If we have chosen to be Christians and know God loves us, **we should never lose hope. He will always be with us; when we ask Him, He will help us work it out**.

Questions to Consider:
1. What would you do if you were in Marcie's situation?_____
2. What do you think might happen if you ran TO a solution (your creditors) rather than away from them?_____
3. What about your situation? Have you looked at it closely? Do you know how much you spend on various items in your 'spending plan?' Would you like to begin working on it? If so, please turn to the next page.

Itemized Monthly Spending Plan:

1. **Gross salary**_____
2. **Tithe** _____
3. **Savings**_____
4. **Estimated Tax**_____
5. **Housing**_____
6. **Food (not eating out)** _____
7. **Auto/truck payment**_____
8. **Insurance**_____
9. **Entertainment/recreation**_____
10. **Clothing**_____
11. **Medical**_____
12. **Miscel (Eating Out)** _____
13. **Investments/retirement**_____
14. **School/childcare**_____

Total Expenses_____

Gross salary minus total expenses_____

The total expenses cannot exceed the salary.

Note 1: Make as many copies of this as needed.

Note 2: If you do not know (like I did in the past) how much you spend in specific categories, a spending diary is recommended.

Use your phone or a small tablet to record each category (especially the problem ones) daily.

Total them up at the end of each week but continue to keep a record until you have at least a full month. If you are like me, you will be quite surprised when you complete this form.

But no wonder. **We are part of a society that has a plan for our money—and <u>that is</u> <u>to take it from us</u>.** We are unwittingly managing our money the world's way.

You might say, how so? The more we watch T.V., the more we look at our computer screens, the more we look at our cell phones**, the more advertising we see**. Then guess what? A certain percentage of us will go out and purchase the item, or, more likely, we will click on it on our cell phones or computers. And BOOM—the item comes in the mail, and the advertiser won!

Just so you know, even though I am fully aware of their nefarious schemes, I am not immune to this. For example, I like certain healthy foods. My computer has learned this, and so nearly every day, I receive ads for the healthy foods I like, and sometimes, I buy them!

But if we are aware of this (as you now are**), knowledge helps us exercise restraint.** We want and need to manage our money properly—for ourselves and for those who depend on us.

So, what should your plan be? Many recommend the 10/10/80 plan. This means you tithe 10% (we will talk more about this later), save 10%, and live on 80%. You might say—that is impossible! And for Marcie, in the example above, it may be initially. But as she and her family seek counsel and gain wisdom in managing their finances, the situation likely will improve.

Life Lesson #2. When one spouse does not do their part.

In 2018, Doug and Margie were barely making it. Bills were getting paid, but there was no surplus, and certainly no emergency fund. Then Doug lost his job. For two long years, he was out of work. Despite Margie's jobs as an executive assistant and a waitress, they could not make ends meet. They refinanced their home to pull out the cash they needed, but nothing else changed. There is no job for Doug, and there are no significant expense cuts. The cash ran out.

Now, they have maxed out 10 credit cards at interest rates ranging from 14.99 percent to 24.75 percent, and their minimum monthly payments total $1700. Their house payment is $ 1,900 per month, and they have two daughters in college. Doug recently found a job as a small-business manager, earning $ 1,650 per month, but the financial hole they are in swallows his salary without him even noticing. They still cannot make it.

Margie's salary (from two jobs in 2019) is $ 3,500 per month, and Doug's is $ 1,650. With the $1700 minimum due on credit cards and the rest of their bills, they have a whopping $ 2000-per-month deficit. What is going to happen?

Knowing that they would not be able to pay their credit cards sometime soon, and one had already been declined, the coach gave them contact information for a credit card agency that could help. When it reduces their interest rates to 9 percent or less, it will lessen their card payments by $500 or more. While helpful, it would only reduce their monthly deficit to $ 1,500. He also suggested that they might need to stop paying for their daughters' college. This, together with other cuts, may allow them to break even. It will be a close call.

Action Steps: While working with a credit agency to reduce their interest rates, Doug and Margie need to have a heart-to-heart with their daughters: they just cannot pay for college now. If the daughters are motivated to continue in school, they should both take on part-time jobs and perhaps cut their class load to what their part-time jobs can cover. Doug needs to accept more responsibility for earning a living. He needs to be reminded of what it says in the Good Book:

> 1 Timothy 5:8 "but if anyone does not provide for his own, and especially for those of his household, he has denied the faith, and is worse than an unbeliever.

Looking more closely into this, I might find that Doug has always been lazy and that his wife has been the 'go-getter.'

But now they are at a breaking point. While Doug continues to search for a better-paying job, **he needs to accept responsibility for preparing meals at home to reduce their reliance on fast food.**

They will probably go bankrupt unless Doug and Margie do everything listed above—and perhaps even more. With counseling, encouragement, and prayer—even if bankruptcy happens—they can still find success. Everyone makes mistakes. The key is to learn from them and keep the marriage intact.

Questions to Consider:

1. If you were Margie, what would you do?_____
2. How would you counsel Doug?_____
3. Do you think they should keep the marriage intact? If so, how would they accomplish that?_____

Life Lesson #3. Judith's son asked her to refinance her home.

Judith called to ask if she should refinance her home to help her son. Early in the conversation, she divulged that she was blind. When asked what the funds would be used for and how they would be repaid, she said she was uncertain about repayment, but she suspected he might use them to purchase another car. Because her son had not conveyed specifically what the money would be used for and, more importantly, how it would be repaid, we can already see that this is unlikely to be a good decision.

A son with a legitimate emergency (which should be the only reason you would call your mother with this request) would say specifically how the money would be allocated and specifically how he would pay it back. With no more information than Judith has, the advice is that her son needs to be independent and not ask his mother to give him something she may need later – equity in her home. He is over twenty-one, an adult needing to take responsibility for himself.

Action Step: In this culture, kids may want to continue to depend on Mom or Dad. They will do so when Mom or Dad allows it, even throughout their adult lives. It is especially tempting if that parent is the only one left. He or she feels sorry for the child and wants to help. The parent has probably spent the last 20-plus years helping the child grow to be an adult. Another mistake easily leads to another bailout. And another.

Extenuating circumstances can change the situation. We are not talking here about children with mental or physical issues that limit their potential; we are talking about normal kids who just do not want to accept the responsibility of adult life.

Some children need more encouragement than others to be ushered out of the nest. Kids who continue to depend on their parents will never mature properly, grow into the men and women God and their parents want them to be, or accomplish the work He has for them.

Questions to Consider:

1. What would you do if you were Judith?_____
2. Do you think it is appropriate for kids, when they have reached adult age, to be encouraged to leave home?_____

Life Lesson #4. Pastor Leon and his new blue pickup truck.

Pastor Leon had always wanted a new truck. His ministry was going well, and when he realized his salary was enough to cover the payments, he headed straight to his favorite dealership, picked out a new blue pickup—the exact model he desired—and bought it. He was as happy as he could be. For about a year.

Suddenly, a trio of unexpected expenses rained down on him. His daughter was getting married. His wife became sick and had to make numerous visits to the doctor. Serious house repairs became evident.

Now there was not enough money to go around. If he did not make his truck payments, the bank would repossess the truck, which would be really embarrassing. His daughter's marriage plans were more expensive than he thought they would be. Who could have guessed that his normally healthy wife would have all these health issues? And why did these things have to happen to his house, especially now at this time?

In God's timing, right in the middle of this crisis, I was scheduled to speak at his church. At his first opportunity, Pastor Leon asked me why God would allow all this to happen when he was trying to do a good work for Him.

Action Step: I answered his question with another question.

"Did you seek counsel and/or pray seriously about the purchase of the truck *before* you bought it?"

"No, I forgot."

"You forgot?"

"Well, actually, it never occurred to me. It just seemed like a simple, logical decision. Either I could afford it, or I could not, and at the time, it seemed like I could."

The pastor forgot that God wants to be involved in every area of our lives, including spending.

> *Luke 16:11 (NIV) "If therefore you have not been faithful in the use of unrighteous mammon (worldly wealth), who will entrust the true riches to you?*

What is God saying here? We must be faithful in how we use our money, which is His money. This includes praying before any purchase and, more seriously, before a major purchase.

If Pastor Leon had specifically prayed before buying the new truck, God may have impressed upon him to wait. Was it a sin for him to buy the truck? No, but only God knows the future. It is in our best interest to ask Almighty God, who knows the future, what to do before the future arrives.

Two other points: First, God is not a fan of debt. Pastor Leon made only a small down payment and borrowed the rest. If he had consulted God's Word, he might have rediscovered God's dislike of debt and felt led to save for a year before making this purchase.

Then he would have avoided the difficulties he was now in.

Second, what kind of 'cushion' did Pastor Leon have? The evidence would suggest he had saved very little. I wonder if he was like the guy in Proverbs:

> *Proverbs 21:20 "The wise man saves for the future, but the foolish man spends whatever he gets."*

The ultimate point: Do not lose hope! Even when we make mistakes that leave us feeling hopeless, we should *never* lose hope. Why? because we know God loves us and has a plan for us. He can and will adjust His plan for us to accommodate our mistakes.

I spoke with Pastor Leon over a year later. After he had gotten serious about prayer and asked God for direction about his finances, God worked miraculously in his life. With God's help, he weathered the abovementioned crises and then focused on paying off his truck. Now he was on his way.

When we focus on what God wants, things will usually get better. And if they do not, they certainly will in heaven when we see Him there.

Questions to Consider:

1. If you were Pastor Leon, would you have jumped at the chance to purchase this truck?_____
2. What should he have done?_____

Life Lesson #5. Ken and his hot muscle car.

A financial coach had a young friend, Ken, who, at 20, wanted a hot muscle car. He did not consider whether it was God's will for him to buy the car; he just wanted a hot car. He found one for $12,000, but with almost no cash to put down, his low-paying job and poor credit made it impossible to get dealer financing. The dealer tried four banks before he found one that would accept the loan, for an additional loan insurance premium of $1,000 and at a higher interest rate.

Ken was thrilled with his hot muscle car. However, after six months, guess what? **He missed a payment!** The bank then began calling him. Rather than minimizing his spending and trying to save money to pay the missed payment, he decided he could manage the financial pressure, so he continued.

Four months later, Ken missed another payment! Now, the bank really began hounding him. Rather than try to pay the missed payment somehow, he took what he thought was the easiest way out—he drove the car to the bank and said, "You want it, so here it is."

He hated losing his treasure, but he could not take the pressure. It was becoming a nightmare, and he wanted it to end.

But it did not end. Not by a long shot. The bank is not a car dealer; it does what it always does: sell the car at the wholesale auction market. This is the quickest and easiest way for them to recoup a portion of their losses. But what did it do for Ken?

Ken had bought the car at retail and paid an additional fee for loan insurance. The bank got much less for it at wholesale, leaving a big gap between what they had loaned and what they got back in payments and wholesale price. They retained their attorney to take Ken to court for the remaining amount due.

You might think this amount due would be reasonable – the difference between retail and wholesale, further reduced by his payments. Not so. Back interest on the loan (at its high interest rate), late, court, and attorney fees totaled about $16,000 in judgment from the court. And this was *after* the bank had gotten the wholesale value of the car!

Ken was shocked and angry. Not about to pay for a car he no longer owned, he declared bankruptcy. Although it felt like a good choice at the moment, it haunted him for ten years. The only vehicles he could buy during that time were ones he could purchase with cash, for less than $500, because that was all he could scrape up. You can imagine the quality of his ride and the ding on his pride.

Note: His coach reports that Ken learned his lesson, has matured, and is now financially responsible. Sometimes we learn the hard way. The key point is to learn.

Action Step: How can we make it without borrowing? What should Ken have done? He should have obtained godly counsel, as in Proverbs 12:15 (see below).

> Proverbs 12:15 *the way of a fool is right in his own eyes, but a wise man is he who listens to counsel.*

Then he would have been told to save as much money as possible before purchasing a less expensive car, so he could at least minimize the amount he borrowed.

One reason the dealer had difficulty obtaining a loan was that Ken could not afford this hot car; it was too expensive for his income. If Ken had to buy a vehicle while unable to pay cash, a less expensive car with a decent down payment would have meant a smaller loan and a smaller payment he could afford.

Ken's next step should have been to pay off the less expensive car quickly. Then he should have kept making payments – but this time to his own bank account – so that when he needed another car (maybe even a used, hot muscle car), his savings plus the value of his present vehicle would allow him to pay for it in full, or as close to it as possible.

As an aside: When the first bank turned down Ken's loan request, he went to his parents and asked them to co-sign. They wisely turned him down. This is discussed in detail in the next lesson, but can you imagine the stress and arguments that would have resulted had Ken's parents given in to his request? This likely would have caused hard feelings that would have lasted for years.

Questions to Consider:

1. Do you think Ken ever attempted to prepare a spending plan? What do you think would have happened if he had?
2. Shortly before turning the car back to the bank, Ken tried to sell it for the $13,000 ($12,000 plus $1,000 for the loan insurance) he had in it. He received an offer of $11,800, which meant he had to come up with $ 1,200. He did not want to do that. Do you think he regrets this decision?
3. **So, how would you apply this situation to you? Do you need another car currently? What are your plans to acquire it?** Some

considerations: If you purchase a new vehicle, you will immediately lose thousands of dollars upon driving it off the dealership lot, because your car's value will be thousands of dollars less. Plus, you will be paying back those thousands with interest unless you pay cash.

If this fits into your budget, it is recommended that you purchase a four- or five-year-old car with relatively low mileage. The lower price will save you the thousands mentioned above, and cars today, when well cared for, can last 200,000 miles or more.

Life Lesson #6. Let's talk about CREDIT

Some financial gurus say that if you have the money, you do not need credit. If you need a car, save the money until you can pay for it in full. **However, there are times, especially when starting out, when you need to rent an apartment, purchase a vehicle with a loan, or even be accepted for a cell phone contract, when you usually need credit.**

How to obtain credit:

1. Go to your local bank and ask them if they have a 'credit builder' program. The program typically

works as follows: You provide the bank with funds for a secured credit card (typically $300 to $1,000). The bank puts those funds in a Secured Certificate of Deposit (CD). The bank then issues you a (secured) credit card, for which you can charge up to the amount of your Secured Certificate of Deposit, i.e., $300. Now you can use the credit card for routine purchases up to $300. The critical part is you MUST pay the minimum amount due BEFORE the due date. However, **it is highly recommended that you pay your card balance in full before each due date**.

2. Why? Why should you pay your card off in full before each due date? The answer: So, you do not owe them interest on their money. **If you pay it in full, then how much does the credit card cost you? NOTHING!**

3. Note: Each time you receive a bill, there will be two numbers on the bill. One number is the **minimum amount** you owe on the card. The second number is the **full amount** you owe on the card. Why do the credit card people offer this? **Because they want you to pay only the minimum amount you owe**. Why do they want you to pay only the minimum amount**? So, they can charge you interest**! Not only this, but they will also charge you HIGH interest—**currently 23% plus**. Now they are taking money from

you—which you do not want because you cannot afford this—if you're going to reach your important financial goals.

4. As an aside, according to Bankrate, as I write this, approximately 44% of all Americans carry a credit card balance from month to month. The average rate they pay is from 23.5% to 24.92%.

5. **The point is that banks are in this to make money from you, but we can beat them at their game by paying the credit card off in full BEFORE it is due. If you pay the total amount due each month, how much does the credit card cost you? <u>NOTHING!</u>**

6. **Important: You and I always need an emergency fund—a cushion — to always have the money to pay your card off in full or to take care of other emergencies. This is the reason to manage your funds using the 10/10/80 concept. Note: There is nothing wrong with having more than a 10% emergency fund—in reality, it should be a fund big enough to take care of us for several months—more about that later.**

7. The point is that you and I want to build a good credit (FICO) score without paying for it. If you do as described, your credit score will increase when you make payments on your bank card on or before they are due, and it will cost you nothing. Yes, maybe you did have to put $300 in

a secured CD, but you will eventually receive all of it back as your credit score improves.

8. Next: to help your score increase faster, you can also open a charge account at another bank and/or you can open up an account at your favorite grocery or computer store. To maximize the increase of your credit score, you could have three cards—IF you use them properly by paying them off in total each month before they are due.

9. **Note: I have heard some recommend you deal only in cash, so you can see the money going in and out**. There is nothing wrong with this system—but it will not assist you with your credit score, which you will probably need to rent an apartment or purchase your first car if using a loan.

10. **Pros and cons of a debit card versus a credit card**: Some financial advisors say that you should use only debit cards because that encourages you to make certain the money is in the bank before you swipe the card. Note: There is nothing wrong with this either, and it is the opposite of the credit card, which allows you to make a purchase and then worry about how you will pay for it later. **But a debit card does not help you build a credit score, unless you use it as a credit card**. You may have heard the story about this guy who was robbed of his debit card

and cell phone. The thief then took the guy's cell phone, texted the wife asking for their security code—she texted it back to him—and he emptied out their bank account. In speaking with a banker, he said that if that happens, after some verification, the bank will refund the money—but still you would have to go through the process. Personally, I like the idea of using someone else's money (from the credit card), knowing the service is free when I pay it back in full every month--and if I lose the card, or if it is stolen, with one phone call I am likely protected, even if the thief has already placed charges on my card.

Questions:

1. Have you completed your budget from page 20?_____
2. Which of the stories do you relate to most in this chapter? _____
3. What actions have you taken, or will take, as a result of reading this chapter? _____
4. What did you like, and/or what did you not like about this chapter?_____

Week 2: Taming Your Financial Excesses

Things do not always work out as planned. I could not imagine running out of fuel on my flight to Gainesville. With a direct flight requiring less than three and a half hours of fuel, what kind of detour could possibly use up the six hours I had on board? Answer: a longer detour than anticipated.

There will be times when we encounter job struggles, health issues, or family emergencies of all kinds. But when we rely on the Lord and seek godly advice, we have a much better chance of discovering His plan for our lives, which should lead to things working out for the best.

Life Lesson #7. What can 'success' look like?

Sometimes you cannot do everything you want (like arriving at Gainesville on time). Mark wanted to be the 'total' provider of the family and give them virtually everything they wanted. The trouble was that Mark could not afford it. He thought he would soon be granted a substantial raise at work to address his overspending. **But the raise did not come, and his spending ran him and his family into a financial wall**.

This scenario usually does not end well, and this one looks that way, too.

The good news is that Mark called his church and asked for advice.

> *Proverbs 12:15..." the wise man is he who listens to counsel."*

He was referred to an excellent coach with biblical knowledge and financial expertise.

When the coach analyzed the situation, it became apparent there was a significant problem. **Mark had two large mortgages on their house and a whopping $200,000 in credit card debt. Ouch!** The card interest alone took all their discretionary income, so there was no money for food. They had to keep borrowing just to put food on the table. This is what a downward spiral looks like! What could they do?

The average person would probably say, "Just declare bankruptcy."

Action Step: The good news is that the coach they called had more wisdom than the average coach. First, he told them that, with God's help, they would not declare bankruptcy. He shared with them the Bible verse, which speaks to this when it says in the Psalms:

> *Psalm 37:21 "the evil man borrows and does not pay back..."*

With the help of one of the agencies listed in the Resource Section (page 134), they could lower the interest rates on the cards and establish a payback plan. But their debts were so high that this still would not accomplish the objective—paying back their debts and having funds to live on. **So, after checking out several attorneys, their coach recommended one who had led them through bankruptcy to lower interest rates beyond what was possible with the agency and to structure a payback plan that would allow them to repay the debts while continuing to live.**

There were still other issues, but as they turned them over to God, He restored them individually. But they had to give them to Him first. They did and were blessed. Isn't it interesting how God wants us to give everything to Him, and then He often gives it all back?

As of this writing, they are three years into their five-year payback plan—which will pay back 98% of their debts. During this year, there have been other miracles. One, for example, concerned their daughter's old car, which she needed for college and work. It died. A friend had a $2,000 car for sale (also old but ran well), but they had no money with which to purchase it, and they could not borrow the funds. What to do?

They prayed. In answer to their prayer, the friend sold them the car with no money down and said, "Just pay what you can, even if it is only $40 per month." He gave them the title and accepted $40 monthly for over six months. Per God's plan, the dad received over $2,000 for a year-end bonus from work, which he used to pay off the car! What a great answer to prayer. What a great God we serve!

Note: This is what success looks like. This family was headed for disaster. They asked for help from the church (God's people). The coach they found helped them turn their situation around—found a way for them to pay off all their debts and still pay their regular living expenses. Now, with God's help, they are headed in the 'right' direction with a bright future ahead. As an aside, think about the testimony this provides for their kids. They will

never forget their father's mistakes and how he humbled himself to God's plan. Even though it was difficult, it worked out for everyone in the end.

Questions to Consider:

1. What would you do if you were Mark and unthinkingly let yourself get into a bind like his?
2. Mark could have kept the year-end bonus of over $2,000 and then kept paying his friend the $40 monthly. Would you have made that decision, or would you have kept your promise and given it to your friend?
3. How would God have worked in their lives if they had declared bankruptcy?

Life Lesson #8. Louann and her medical bills.

Louann called. "My husband, Roddy, and I want to buy a house next year, but we have a problem. Four years ago, I had a medical issue that left me with $10,000 in past-due medical bills. We haven't paid for any of these, and our credit score has taken a hit."

"Ouch," the coach said. Before he could say anything else, Louann continued.

"It gets worse. Two of the organizations recently sent their bills to a collection agency. Now our credit score is tanking even more. Is there any hope for us trying to buy a home?"

"Of course, there is, Louann," the coach said, racking his brain to figure out what to say next. "It will probably take longer than the twelve months you're hoping for, but it can happen in due time."

"Thank you," she said. "That's a relief. But why should it have to take longer than a year?"

Wanting to be both forthright and sensitive, the coach said, "First, let me say how sorry I am that you had a medical issue. No one plans for that, and it can seem so unfair when you have not only physical issues but also unexpected bills. Unfortunately, it's a reality that can hit anyone, and we must deal with it. Fortunately, we have God's help when we respond in His way."

"So, what *is* His way?" she asked.

The coach dug into the facts of their situation, including their spending plan. "It's good to see that you have stayed current with all of your other bills," he said. "At least these medical bills are the exception. The biggest problem is that you have just ignored them for over four years because you mentally put them in a different category – unexpected, unwanted, and unfair. But this doesn't satisfy the obligation."

"I just don't have the money," she said.

"This might seem like a strange question," the coach said, "but how do you feel about the amount in your spending plan that you are giving to your church?"

"I think it's all I can afford, and actually, we're not even giving that amount regularly. We're kind of hit-and-miss with it. But back to the medical bill question," she continued, "Roddy doesn't want to have anything to do with them."

"You mean he doesn't think they need to be paid?"

"Not exactly. He just thinks that I have a good salary, these are my bills, and I should be responsible for paying them. His money is his to spend his way, and he feels like he pays his fair share of our regular household bills."

Doesn't this situation sound like an accident waiting to happen?

Fortunately, Roddy was willing to speak to the coach about managing his finances God's way. He listened and learned some Scriptures applicable to his situation. The first was,

> *Psalm24:1 "The earth is the Lord's, and all it contains, the world, and those who dwell in it,"*

In other words, God owns everything, including the money he thought was his own.

The second was:

> *Luke 16:11, "If therefore you have not been faithful in the use of unrighteous mammon [worldly wealth], who will entrust the true riches to you?"*

In other words, how you spend "your" money impacts your relationship with God and obtaining the 'true riches.'

Roddy began to have second thoughts about keeping "his" money separate. As many couples are, they were united in marriage but not in money.

After considering managing "his" money God's way rather than his own, he realized his error and was willing to cooperate with his wife. Note: This speaks volumes about this man's character. He was willing to humble himself, see the truth in God's Word, and change. Roddy is becoming a true man of God.

Action Steps: Following their conversations with the coach, Louann and Roddy began working together on a unified spending plan that includes a tithe to their church and allocates funds for hospital bills.

Their next step is to contact each medical company they owe money to and explain their situation: their income, their other obligations, and the amount they can afford to pay on hospital bills. If each creditor receives some money, they may be able to reach an agreement.

However, if the companies do not cooperate, Louann and Roddy might need to work with one of the credit companies listed on page 144. These companies have options that are not available to the average person. They charge for their services, but usually, the savings outweigh the costs.

Another consideration: Even though Louann and Roddy could declare bankruptcy over the $10,000 medical bills, it would be foolish. At this time, declaring bankruptcy damages a person's credit for ten years. This means it would be difficult and likely delay their ability to obtain a mortgage for a house. It could also result in the lender assigning them a higher rate.

How do we think God views bankruptcy? We know He wants us to be honest and to pay our bills. We incurred them; they are ours to pay. It says in the Psalms

> Psalms 37:21 *"The wicked borrows and does not pay back, . . ."*

We also know that God will hold us accountable for our actions as believers. As a couple who follow God, Louann and Roddy must do everything they can to pay their bills.

Having taken these steps, Louann and Roddy's future looks good, especially since they are both on board with the plan.

One of the experienced coaches on our team said, "I have never had a plan fail when both parties were truly on board with it. Together, they have always worked it out." This is evidence of the power of a team, especially a team with the Lord on its side. Louann and Roddy will be able to purchase a house in due time.

Although this is too late for Louann and Roddy, there is another option for those with large hospital bills they cannot or will have difficulty paying. **Most hospitals are not-for-profit**. To justify and maintain this status, these hospitals are obliged to provide some free services to the poor. **Suppose Louann and Roddy had approached the hospital <u>within 30 days after</u> receiving their initial statement showing the amount due, and explained their situation. In that case, it is possible the hospital would have reduced its debt by a sizeable percentage or even forgiven it entirely.** However, to accomplish this, they had to contact the hospital shortly after receiving the bill.

This is an important point for anyone in this predicament to consider. It also emphasizes the urgency of running TO our creditors, not from them.

Questions to Consider:

1. What would you have done if you were Louann or Roddy?
2. Medical bills are extremely expensive now. Are there options to minimize them? What are they? See the above paragraph for one example.

Life Lesson #9. Marty was afraid to tell her husband.

Marty wrote:

> I am paying off a credit card consolidation at $220 a month. I have eleven more payments. The bad thing is that I pay the bills and then collect my husband's share from him. It is hard to keep enough in my account to pay for it. I get hit with fees when he is slow. I should have savings, but now I have $15,000 in additional credit card debt. I have little to show for it because I put our family's vacation weekends on it.

Please don't think I am blaming my husband. He is frugal, but I am not. He has savings, and he thinks I do too. It will break his heart if I tell him, and I am afraid he will divorce me. I make $85,000 a year, but I will retire in two years. Also, should I transfer the $15,000 to another card? Please help.

The coach's response to Marty was:

I am so sorry you are in this fix. Obviously, this has been building for years. The fact that you have contacted me makes me think you must be a Christian. I am thankful for that and hopeful that your husband is as well.

Honestly, the first thing you need to do is tell your husband. He will be disappointed and may get mad, even stay mad for several days, but if he is a Christian, he most likely will not divorce you.

The second thing you need to do is pray about this – together. This is too big for you to do alone. Together, you need to set up a plan (God's plan for you), and then both of you adhere to it.

> Proverbs 12:15 "...the wise man/woman is he/she who listens to counsel."

There is a company (see page 144) that can help negotiate lower interest rates, maybe even lowering them all down to 9 percent or less. You are probably now paying 18 to 25 percent. They will charge you a $30-50 monthly fee, but you will save much more on interest.

You asked whether you should transfer balances to another card. If that card charges less than 9 percent interest, it could be a good option—if your husband agrees.

I have prayed for you, and I pray that everything works out well in the end. Thank you for contacting this ministry.

Marty's response:

"Oh, thank you! I am praying too! Thank you for being so gracious to me. I will call the company right away. I'm very excited about resolving this. I cut up my cards and froze the accounts. God bless you. Thank you for assisting me as a brother would. You cannot believe the relief I'm feeling right now."

Coach's response:

It is always good to be appreciated!

Action Step: Marty was caught up in her situation and could not see a way out. All of us need godly counsel at times. It is important to humble ourselves in the situation and seek the counsel God has waiting for us.

Questions to Consider:

1. Was the coach correct in suggesting that Marty tell her husband?
2. What would you do if you were in this situation?
3. Was her idea to cut up her cards and freeze the accounts a good choice?
4. Initially, she paid off her cards using a **consolidation loan**. Was this a good idea? See Life Lesson #10 next.

Life Lesson #10. Donald and his <u>Consolidation Loan</u> request.

Donald called his coach. "I've been a long-distance truck driver most of my life. It's something I know and do well. But on the other hand, I do some other things, which haven't turned out so well. I guess I didn't know as much about them as I thought. One of them was investing in gold."

Note: There is nothing wrong with investing in gold or silver. Gold and silver have been money for 4,000-plus years. The U.S. Dollar was backed by gold until President Nixon took the country off the gold standard in 1971. Some people say gold and silver are relics of money and should be forgotten. However, since 2001, gold has gone from about $271 per ounce to nearly $5,000 per ounce as of 2026. This is a 1754% gain over 25 years (an average of more than 70% per year). Gold and silver can be good investments.

What did Donald do? He borrowed money on his credit cards to buy gold, expecting the price to rise at the time. But then gold went from $1,800 per ounce to $1,400. Now he is stuck. The bad part is that Donald borrowed almost $50,000 on credit cards at an average interest rate of 18 percent.

Donald's first mistake was borrowing money to invest. This is rarely a good idea, and borrowing at a high interest rate is even worse. He now has a monthly obligation of $1,000 plus.

Note: There is no guaranteed investment. All investments have issues and may not provide the return we expect. See Chapter 6 for further discussion of investment. **Debts, however, will not go away unless we do something unscriptural**, such as declaring bankruptcy, placing us under its own penalties and restrictions.

"One other thing," he said. **"I recently got a call from a consolidation company.** They said they would cut my credit card debt by almost half, and I would have only one low payment. **What do you think? Should I do this?"**

The problem with consolidation loans is that borrowers can have zero balances on their credit cards (or, in Donald's case, half) and immediately return to their old habit of running up **charges. Then, they would have both the credit card bills and their new consolidation loan to repay, which would cause their credit score to take a significant hit.**

The company offered to write off almost half of Donald's credit card balances because it felt it would be better to take a 50 percent loss than a 100 percent loss.

When someone like Donald needs a consolidation loan, it generally means he has lost control of his spending, exhausted his normal credit options, and now needs additional credit. In Donald's case, since he could not pay his credit card bills, it appeared that he needed a consolidation loan and a discharge or write-off of some of his debts.

The answer to Donald's question above is--a consolidation loan would seem the easy solution. However, it would significantly damage his credit, and from God's point of view, per the verse in Psalms:

> *Psalms 37:21 says, "The wicked borrows and does not pay back..."*

He should pay the $50,000 back.

Finally, Donald has documented that he did not know how to invest in gold and rushed into it. In his initial conversation about the past, he said there were other things he had rushed into. Paying back the entire $50,000 will take Donald some time. In that time, he will perhaps learn the lessons God has for him, lessons that will make him less likely to repeat his mistakes in the future.

Every one of us has weaknesses. God, in His sovereignty, knows our weaknesses and has a plan to overcome them.

We need to follow His plan so we will grow as His adopted children into the mature Christians He wants us to be.

If Donald decides not to take the consolidation option, he should call one of the credit card companies listed in the Resource Section on page 144. They will likely assist him in significantly reducing the interest rate for a small monthly charge. Given his large balances, the cost should be well worth it.

Initially, Donald would have been better off using just the cash he had on hand to purchase his gold. Then, he could have waited until it went up (perhaps years), giving him the potential for a large profit.

Questions to Consider:

1. What would you do if you were in Donald's situation? _____
2. Do you believe the coach gave Donald the correct advice?_____
3. Is this the advice God would have given him? Or would you recommend that Donald take the consolidation loan offer?_____
4. Proverbs 21:5 says, "...*hasty (speculation) comes surely to poverty.*" Does this apply here?_____
5. In this chapter, which stories did you relate to the most?_____

Week 3: Need vs Want--The Ultimate Showdown

Life Lesson #11. How to deal with cosigning.

This is a frequent question: What if my 18-year-old son or daughter needs a cosigner for their first car since they have not yet established credit?

Let's go first to the Bible.

> *Proverbs 22:26-27 "Do not be among those who give pledges [cosign], among those who become guarantors for debts. If you have nothing with which to pay, why should he take your bed from under you?"*

> *Proverbs 17:18 "A man lacking in sense pledges and becomes guarantor in the presence of his neighbor"*

God warns us not to cosign or guarantee someone's debts in these Scriptures.

But what if we still want/need to pursue the co-signing? **What if the child is insistent and the adult feels they have no choice in their situation**? What do we need to consider as they purchase their first car, which they think we need to co-sign for?

1. **If they do not make the payments, can we afford to make them**? Note: Many parents believe their child when he/she says he/she has a good job and nothing will go wrong. But as you will see in the example below, and as adults, we intuitively know that things sometimes do go wrong. Therefore, the question of whether we can afford the payments is a realistic one and needs to be carefully analyzed.
2. **If we are required to make the payments, will this damage our relationship with our child?**
    - Will resentment show in our conversations?
    - Could we still speak with them about important decisions such as a career, a possible spouse, or, even more importantly, their relationship with God

and influence them to walk closely with Him?

The answers to these questions should determine our answer to our child.

However, what happens when we do not know or do not consider those questions?

Jacqueline and her daughter Josephine (they called her Josie) found this out the hard way.

It all started years ago when Jacqueline disagreed with her father, Frank. Frank had instructed her, over and over, on the correct way to manage her money as a young child. When she began her first real job and was earning good money, still living at home, he sat her down and provided an outline of what she should do and some investments she should make.

She disagreed with her dad and was not willing to put money into an investment. To her, this would be a sacrifice, and she wanted nothing of it. When she married, her husband also made good money, and they had the same philosophy—let's enjoy it.

Fast forward 20 years. Jacqueline and her husband now have an 18-year-old daughter. Her daughter, Josie, needs a car. But Josie does not want just any car; she wants a new, classy car, like that of her rich friends. Even her mother thought this was 'over the top.' Unfortunately, guess who won out? Josie.

The other, bigger issue, even though Josie had a job, is that it was not enough of a job to justify this car.

The car dealer said, "No problem, Josie. Have your mother sign this form, and we will put you behind the wheel!" Josie was so excited she could hardly sit still.

The good news is that Jacqueline and Josie had a wonderful relationship. Jacqueline had raised her daughter to be like her, and she was. They agreed on most things, and as many mothers and daughters are, they were close. So, when Josie asked her to sign this co-sign form, even though she had misgivings, she did not want to disappoint her daughter and believed her when she promised she would make those payments.

However, six months later, it is March 2020. Covid-19 has dealt the economy a serious blow, and **Josie has lost her job.** To further complicate matters, Jacqueline had no savings to speak of, and of all the things she had considered, making her daughter's car payments was not one of them.

When the bank called Jacqueline to tell her she needed to make this payment, she immediately called Josie.

"Honey," she said, "you have got to get a job. I do not care what kind of job it is; even if it is a fast-food job, you have to take it."

"Mom, you cannot mean this! You want me to get a fast-food job?!"

Josie had always considered herself above fast-food jobs, and now her mother was asking her to do this!

This conversation went from bad to worse. The mother and daughter, who had always agreed, were not only disagreeing but disagreeing sharply.

Whether or not the bank would actually repossess this car was irrelevant. What was relevant was that the bank was calling Jacqueline. Jacqueline had good credit, but she did not have much in savings, and this could seriously damage her credit. Josie needed to take responsibility here and do something!

Josie did end up getting a job, and it was not fast food. Unfortunately, it was not soon enough, and because she could not get enough hours, it did not pay enough. To prevent her credit from being damaged, Jacqueline and her husband scraped the funds together to make the payments. Josie made most of the payment, however it was over a month late, and the next payment was even later. Jacqueline's calls to Josie were initially ignored; now they are blocked.

Josie has a job, but it does not pay as much as her previous job did. Not only is Josie now behind on three or more payments, but when she makes a payment, it is not a full payment. This means she is continually falling farther and farther behind.

It has been almost a year. The close mother-daughter relationship is gone. Both are hurt, and both have dug in their heels about what they feel is right. Neither of them feels they can give in. They have not spoken in months.

Action Steps: When two people who are close come to a deadlock such as this, the hurt feelings are worse. They were so close, now they are so far apart.

If they attend a church and both parties are willing, this author suggests they make an appointment with the appropriate counselor and discuss this fully.

Let's consider some options: First, can Jacqueline and her husband financially make Josie's car payments? If they can and choose to, this will restore the relationship to some degree. Forgiveness, demonstrated sacrificially, can have a powerful impact.

However, if they cannot afford it or want to practice tough love, they could stop paying for the car. This would force the bank to repossess the car and perhaps permanently damage the mother-daughter relationship. It might also teach Josie to be more cautious financially, a lesson she would never forget.

The best solution might be for them to agree that the mother pay half (for example) of the car payment, and Josie pay the other half. This would also show the mother's forgiveness and go a long way toward repairing their relationship.

If I did the above and this was my son, I might insist I have the spare key so that if he did not make the agreed payment, I could personally repossess the car.

The point is that borrowing money is risky. It poses a threat to our financial stability, emotional health, and often our relationships. That's why God is so specific about what we should and shouldn't do. We need to pay attention to His guidance.

Questions to Consider:

1. What would you do if you were Jacqueline?
2. What would you do if you were Josie?
3. Based on the Scripture, Proverbs 17:18, listed at the beginning of this chapter, what do you think God would have them do now?

Life Lesson #11b. How to avoid co-signing.

If we go back to Life Lesson #6, Ken's parents answered wisely by refusing his request to co-sign. My wife and I adopted two little boys in 1998. When they reached driving age, I had to process these questions myself. My response? I declined to cosign in both cases. How did I solve the problem of providing them with vehicles?

First, my wife and I could not afford to purchase expensive vehicles for them. **We prayed and asked God to assist us**. It so happened (God's timing) that a close friend mentioned in passing that because of his father-in-law's senility, he and his wife needed to 'relieve' him of his vehicle. However, there was a problem: the car was damaged in an accident. As it was a nice, still-very-drivable car, I asked if I could test-drive it. I did, and I made them an offer, which they accepted. I liked this car well enough to have the damage repaired and made it my car. Now I could give our older son my old car.

Two years later, we needed to do something for the youngest. Again, in the Lord's timing, my wife's nephew was upgrading his car. But to do that, he needed to unload his old car. What price to pay? The good news is that the car had been damaged by hail and that an insurance claim was pending. We bought the car with the claim pending. The claim worked out to a very reasonable price because we chose not to repair the minor hail damage.

As an aside, because our youngest was rebellious and would not cooperate with our rules, the car sat for a full year (until he was 17) before he was allowed to drive it. Then, when he finally obtained his license and began driving, he pointed out that 'most' of his friends had new or almost-new cars and said their parents had outright given them to them.

"Dad," he said, "won't you even co-sign?"

"No," I said, "I cannot."

"Why?"

"Because God tells me not to, in Proverbs."

He went to his room, mad, but calmed down later.

Mean dad? I don't think so. After all, he now has his own car. If he wants a better one, he can work, save, and buy it. This should motivate him to do just that.

Have I been asked to co-sign on other occasions? Oh yes, as recently as a few weeks ago. Thankfully, Proverbs again gave me the answer I needed.

Questions to Consider:

1. Would you have made the decision I chose to make, or would you have co-signed for a nicer car?_____
2. Have you prayed about something similar and had God work in your life in a positive way?
_____

Life Lesson #12. Johnny Bedford, the construction worker.

Johnny Bedford is a ministry leader at the church that my friend Karen attends. One Sunday, he stopped Karen at church and humbly shared a confession.

"I need help. My finances are a mess. I don't think I spend much, but I don't have any money and can't save. I have no idea where my money is going."

"If you are serious about this," Karen said, "get a receipt for everything you spend, and record it on these sheets." She handed him a few spending diary sheets. "Happy recording," she said with a smile.

They met a month later. The shock seemed permanently etched in his face. "I can't believe how much I spend in convenience stores!"

Working long hours with frequent stops at convenience stores for food, drinks, and snacks, it was as if his pockets had big holes in them. At least he now knows where his money is going.

Johnny now needs to prepare an income-and-expense guideline for himself. For more information, see the sample in the Resource Section.

Johnny also needs to purchase food at a grocery store and prepare his lunches and snacks at home BEFORE he leaves the house, so that he has them with him and does not need to stop at convenience

stores. Convenience stores may be convenient, but they are also very expensive.

Questions to Consider:

1. Do you know anyone who doesn't know where their money is going?
2. How can they correct this problem?
3. What does Luke 16:11 say about this?
4. See the Resource Section for an example of a monthly income and spending sheet.

Life Lesson #13. Janice and her $9,000 credit card debt.

What do we do if we follow God's leading and cannot pay our bills? A single woman, Janice, called for advice about her $9,000 credit card debt. Things had not worked out well in her recent job. Rather than remain in a demanding situation, she prayed about it and felt God leading her to begin her own business. She was so excited that she immediately resigned from her present position. But with no job to cover her living expenses, she began living on her credit cards. Now she was in debt.

Note: Just because Janice felt God was leading her to resign, this did not mean she needed to resign right then.

However, she continued to pray and seek advice. This led to a confidence that God wanted her to begin her own business, Fair Trade Commerce, dedicated to helping African villages create and build businesses. Exciting as it was, there was a problem. Although she was able to get her new business up and running, it was not making enough to cover her current expenses, much less pay down the cards. What should she do?

The first thing Janice needs to understand is that God has an answer for every financial problem. However, **His answer will rarely be to go into debt.**

I have had people say, "I know God wanted me to have *this* house because I prayed about it and qualified for the loan."

"Wait a minute," I say. "There are times I see good people facing eviction because they assumed that if they could get a mortgage, it was proof that they could afford the house – or that God was putting His stamp of approval on it. But even though their intentions were good, they were making a huge mistake. They wanted to buy, the seller wanted them to buy, the real estate agent wanted them to buy, the loan officer wanted them to buy – all of this feels like a tidal wave of confirmation, but it can also be a trap." See also Life Lesson #21.

"So, what do you recommend? Just keep renting?"

"No, a husband and wife must pray seriously about their finances. **They must maintain a healthy margin between their anticipated income and obligations**. Their income can go down or even away in a heartbeat, but the debt collector keeps knocking. With that in mind, they need to decide how much of a mortgage God wants them to have (His plan for them) and then stay inside that limit – regardless of how attractive a more expensive house might be."

Action Steps: The same principle applies to Janice. She may very well feel called to start this new business, but that does not mean she should rely on it as her sole source of support, especially in the beginning. Similarly, it does not mean she should use debt to support herself. Scriptures that apply here are:

> 1 Corinthians 7:23 "You were bought with a price; do not become slaves of men."
>
> Proverbs 22:7 "The rich rules over the poor, and the borrower becomes the lender's slave."

The coach advised Janice to find a way to support herself now, even if it meant working full-time at another job. She could operate the new business part-time until it can meet her financial needs, including paying down her cards. Most new businesses fail because they are undercapitalized: the owners try to take too much cash out too early when they need to put more cash in.

If Janice follows her coach's advice, her finances can be healthy again. And her new business can build on a solid foundation. There is even a greater advantage: Janice can teach African villagers how to build their businesses correctly – from her own experience.

Questions to Consider:

1. What would you do if you were in Janice's position?
2. What better decisions do you think she should have made?

Life Lesson #14. What to do with an arrogant husband.

Valarie is a teacher, and her husband is a healthcare manager. And now they have four children. They are not getting along because of arguments over money.

Recently, he cut up her credit cards, saying, "You spend more than we can afford." They have student loans totaling over $40,000, primarily for his education. In addition, he is a nut about being in good physical shape, so he belongs to an expensive gym. Finally, he thinks it is *his* money. Where are they headed? If this keeps up, they are headed for a separation because she is so frustrated.

Action Step: Since Valarie's husband is convinced she is spending too much and takes the "I am boss" approach by cutting up her cards, she needs evidence of how she is spending the money. The coach recommended that she keep receipts for everything she spends. Ideally, she would categorize them and total the categories.

Then she could sit down with him, show him the receipts and category totals, and say: **"Where do you want me to cut?"**

When she completes this process, whether they agree or not, their communication will be improved. She will have documented her defense, and his respect for her will have increased. Hopefully, this will result in new habits, which are certainly needed in this situation.

Furthermore, she needs to make it clear that it is *their* money. She is working too, and it is *their* children and *their* house, correct?

But even this does not go far enough. Both need to realize it is God's money; the children are God's (a gift from Him); and the house is God's. As we discussed earlier, it says in the Psalms:

> Psalms 24:1 "The earth is the Lord's, and all it contains. . ."

In this case, the coach could not speak with the husband, but it appeared he needed at least an attitude change.

Questions to Consider:

1. What would you do in this situation if you were Valarie?
2. What would be the best method of dealing with a husband (or wife) who exhibited this kind of arrogance?
3. What would you do in this situation if you were the husband?
4. How much of the spending problem was his fault, and how much was her fault?

Life Lesson #15. Gladys and her adult children.

Gladys attended a class called Navigating Your Finances God's Way and said, "I need help." It was a truthful statement. She brought along a list of bills she needed to pay, and it seemed endless.

"When I am stressed," she said, "which is often, I just refuse to open the envelopes with bills. I don't want to see them."

"Do you really do that?" one of the other students asked in disbelief.

"I really do!" she said. Gladys needed to get control of her life. She needed to create new habits and desperately needed a good job. Nearly as important, she needed to learn to deal with her adult children.

Gladys had a 30-year-old son with a dog still living at home and relying on Mom. She also had a daughter who frequently needed money and depended on Mom as well. In her regular phone calls to her class leader, he would stress that she was hurting her adult children by not encouraging them to support themselves.

As Gladys studied in class, she learned that God created work for us, and that work is good for everyone, including her children. She began to realize what she was allowing to happen; her children were remaining children. They needed to

grow up, and she needed to take some action to encourage it.

One of the verses we studied in class was from Colossians. It says,

> *Colossians 3:23-24 "Whatever you do, do your work heartily, as for the Lord rather than for men . . . It is the Lord Christ whom you serve."*

The main message of this verse is that the Lord wants us to work hard and be diligent in our jobs instead of just doing the minimum to get by. He wants us to understand that we are not only working for ourselves or our supervisors but for Him. He is our true boss.

In his book *Your Money Counts*, Howard Dayton tells the carpenter's story. He says, "Just as the carpenter builds the house, so the house builds the carpenter. It refines his skills and teaches him patience and perseverance. He is a better person *after* building the house than before. Work was good for him."

When we realize this, it changes our approach to work. It was important for Gladys to understand that her children needed to learn this. However, by continually allowing them to rely on her for help – whether for a place to live or money because they were spending it unwisely – her children were missing crucial life lessons. They were missing lessons in accountability and taking responsibility for themselves. They were also missing lessons learned at work, such as refining skills, learning patience, and perseverance. These were lessons they needed to become the godly man and woman that she and the Lord wanted them to become.

As noted above, Gladys desperately needed a good job. She had inadvertently allowed her children to interfere with her obtaining it. The class prayed for her, and for a while, it seemed it would never happen. Time passed without results, and she just borrowed more on her student loan and took another course. But the class kept praying.

A year later, she called her leader. She was excited and said, "I have a great job." She wanted to know how much to contribute to her IRA because the company matched 5%. Her leader said, "If you can afford it, put in five percent." Sometimes, our Lord waits to answer a prayer; sometimes, the answer is no. But sometimes it is yes. Either way, we trust and praise Him.

Action Step: Gladys was stuck in her lifestyle. Unwittingly, she let her adult children control her life. As a result, she could never keep a good job, and things never seemed to work out. But with the Lord's help through studying His Word, godly counsel from those in her class, and her effort to

create new habits, she was able to see her situation from a different perspective and break free from it.

Questions to Consider:

1. Have you ever been in a situation like Gladys and her children?
2. What do you think she should have done?
3. What would God's plan for her have been?

Life Lesson #16. Gloria asked what to do about her son.

"James just spends too much," Gloria said. "He has been irresponsible financially and in other ways for years. He is still living at home, and bill collectors are calling. He graduated from the highly touted Christian high school near us, but has always been a rebel. What should I do? Could a coach speak with my son?"

If he is a rebel and will not listen, what good would it do for a coach to talk to him? James did not accept what the expensive Christian education taught him. He neither accepted nor heeded what his mother and father said. He is like the first person in Proverbs 12:15,

> Proverbs 12:15, **"the way of a fool is right in his own eyes**, but a wise man is he who listens to counsel."

or the second person in Proverbs 21:20 (TLB),

> Proverbs 21:20 (TLB) *"The wise man saves for the future,* **but the foolish man spends whatever he gets."**

Gloria needs to be careful not to enable James in any manner. We shouldn't assume that she has in the past; some kids just grow up being rebels. But rather than let these kids fail, it is natural to want to step in and save them from their various misfortunes. It is important for Gloria *not* to step in and save this young man. He has shown he will not learn the 'easy' way, so she needs to let him learn the 'hard' way—the only way he will learn.

The world is a hard taskmaster. It will knock us down repeatedly until we learn. There is one caveat: If a child's life is in danger, we would obviously step in and help. We would also obtain professional counsel.

Action Step: If Gloria and the boy's father step back and let the school of hard knocks teach him these important life lessons, his future looks promising.

Rebels are strong-willed individuals who often achieve great things when they finally head in the right direction.

The challenge is to allow them to endure the hard knocks so they can learn. When James suffers the consequences of his actions, he may be open to counsel and willing to form new habits. If his parents have not burned their bridges in frustration with him, he may even take *their* good counsel and become the man of God they have prayed for.

Questions to Consider:
1. What would you do if James were your son?_____
2. Do you think the advice given above is the correct advice? Is this what God would have wanted someone to say?_____

Week 4: This Is Not Working!

Carelessness can put our marriages at risk. I believe this is especially true with us guys. We can be so obtuse, so focused on our jobs or other concerns, that we do not pay attention to the most important things, such as our wives' feelings.

Relating this to my flight to Georgia, I was so intent on getting to the meeting that I was careless with fuel management. In retrospect, **I feel God was testing me. I clearly did <u>not</u> pass this test. I needed retraining, and He supplied it.**

> *Proverbs 17:3 says. ". . .the Lord tests hearts."*

He sometimes lets us go our own way to see just what we are about. When left to our own ways, what will we do? Will we turn to Him? Will we seek His ways rather than the world's?

Life Lesson #17. Jerome's concern about his wife's spending.

Jerome and his wife both have good jobs. They moved to a better location two years ago, which resulted in a large mortgage. They also have two car payments. His will be paid off next year, and he plans to use those funds to pay off hers more quickly. They carry $85,000 in college debt, which will be paid off in 22 years. He also has a child support obligation for the next nine years.

Jerome has worked out the budget, so they have what they need, but there is not a lot of extra. The problem is that his wife spends extra. Going out with her friends regularly exceeds the budget by over $100. In addition, she often purchases gifts, occasionally expensive ones, for her friend's children. Jerome has spoken to her about this, but either she does not understand or does not care. What should he do?

There is much we do not understand about this situation. For example, why might she not care? Does she believe he doesn't care about her? Are there communication problems? It would be surprising if she didn't understand, but it remains possible. Is she caring for her friend's children because she doesn't have her own? Are other issues, like her husband's child support, causing her resentment? Did he fail to communicate with her when preparing the budget? Does she see it as "his" budget rather than "ours"? Does she think I work hard to earn good money so I can spend it as I wish? Does she believe he is hiding income, as another wife has suggested? Are things truly as tight as he claims?

Action Step: This marriage situation is perhaps tenuous. According to Larry Burkett (deceased) of Christian Financial Concepts and Crown Financial Ministries, 60 percent of marriages that end in divorce point to money problems as a main contributor. Jerome, having already suffered one divorce, does not want this marriage to be financially stressed.

Jerome's coach recommended taking his wife out to dinner some evening and carefully bringing up the issue of their spending plan. **Rather than telling her what to do about it, he needs to ask her what she thinks about it**. Does she think it is necessary? Is it too restrictive? If they can reach an understanding of the importance of having a spending plan, he will have made great progress.

At an appropriate time and in an appropriate manner, he needs to be completely open about his income, her income, and their expenses. At this stage, **it is just**

information—no criticism, no recommendations, no insinuations of any kind.

Another couple had a similar issue. The wife said she could not understand the spreadsheets her husband presented. So, together with the coach, they prepared a basic sheet showing the monthly income at the top, itemized expenses and monthly bills in the middle, and totals at the bottom. It became glaringly obvious that their expenses were hundreds of dollars more than their income – every month. This was not a question of whether cuts needed to be made; it was a question of how deep and in what categories. In this case, the wife really did not want to know or understand the budget. She was just using confusion as an excuse to cover her overspending, which was the biggest part of the problem.

Jerome, over the next few weeks and months, needs to demonstrate how much he cares for his wife. When he does this and resists getting angry over little things, he develops a platform from which to bring up the subject of working on their spending plan. Incidentally, calling this a "spending plan" tends to be more acceptable than calling it a "budget."

Howard Dayton gives a great example in his classes. He says, "us guys" should see "every request from our wives as an opportunity to serve." This is a powerful way to show how much we care. When we demonstrate our care for our wives, it often encourages them to consider something we care about, like a spending plan. As a side note, showing how much we care is something we need to do throughout our lives, whether or not there are problems in the marriage. The book of Colossians addresses this when it says,

> Colossians 3:19 "...husbands, love your wives, and do not be embittered against them."

If Jerome follows the advice here, his future with his wife should be good. Communication is always a potential problem in any marriage, but the future should be bright when good communication is achieved.

Questions to Consider:

1. Do you agree with the coach's recommendations for Jerome?
2. What about his wife? Do you think her actions were justifiable? What would you tell her?

Life Lesson #18 A test in Adam and Jenny's marriage.

Jenny, recently out of the US Navy, now had a full-time job. Her husband, Adam, also worked full-time. With a solid income, they signed a lease on a nice apartment, and things looked promising. But then everything took a turn for the worse. Due to changes at the company where Jenny worked, she lost her job. Ouch!

Then Adam suffered an injury at work. His left shoulder, which had a history of injuries, was injured again. It was becoming apparent that his physically demanding warehouse job might not be a good fit even after his shoulder healed.

Adam and Jenny no longer have the funds necessary to put food on the table and pay their rent, car payments, and other necessities.

"All this bad stuff happened after I came home from the Navy," Jenny said. "Is this an indication we should not stay married? Maybe I should go back into the Navy."

Fortunately, they chose to take positive action. First, they moved in with another couple who were good friends and dedicated Christians. Jenny helped by caring for the children—hers and the other couple's—while the other wife worked. Adam, despite his damaged shoulder, assisted by repairing a car for their friends.

Their next step, prompted by their friends' suggestion, was to start attending the local church with them. Coincidentally, the church was advertising the opening of financial education classes at the right time. Adam was eager to enroll, seeing it as a positive move to address Jenny's question about whether they should even stay married.

During the discussion time in their first class, talkative Jenny shared some specifics of their situation and how desperate they were. Connor, the leader of their small group, understood the gravity of their situation and asked if they would consider further coaching. They said yes, and Conner set a time to meet with them privately.

Coaching uncovered more issues, including one they had never recognized. Because they had never surrendered their hearts to the One True God, they were not walking with Him, trusting in Him, or following His plan for their lives. But faced with the truth, they were willing to start fresh.

In the privacy of the church's coaching room, they knelt together with Connor and prayed. They asked Jesus, whom God sent to be our Savior, to come into their hearts and be their Lord and Savior. They committed their lives to Him, asking for His forgiveness, His saving grace, His guidance, and His help with their specific problems.

In God's miraculous timing, Jenny quickly found another job. Although it was only part-time, her supervisor said it could be turned into a full-time position, and Adam was able to stay home and take care of the children. The next piece of good news was that Adam's workers' compensation came through. After Adam's shoulder had healed sufficiently, he was assigned a desk job, allowing him to get back to work.

The final thing on their list was to get back into an apartment of their own again. At the last report, they were still praying about that. By far the biggest blessing was their newfound peace through hope in the Lord.

Jenny said, "With my new commitment to Jesus our Lord and the promises He has for us, I felt like I had found the family I had always hoped for."

What a wonderful statement. This captures what the church should be—a family.

Action Steps: At a friend's request, they attended church. The local church ministered to them and helped them establish a relationship with their Lord and Savior, Jesus, the Son of God. Then, the Lord Jesus worked in their lives, aiding with their financial struggles and saving their marriage.

Questions to Consider:

1. If you were Adam or Jenny, what would you have done?
2. At one point, Jenny was almost ready for a divorce. What should Adam have done or said?
3. What should they do now? Do you have any recommendations for them?

Life Lesson #19. Brianna says she has no peace.

When Brianna called her coach, she said, "My finances are difficult, I am depressed, I am not healthy, and I need guidance."

When asked to clarify further, she mentioned that she had been married for ten years, divorced for three, and is now married to Thomas, and she doesn't want to do anything to jeopardize this new marriage. However, she remains unsatisfied.

Specifically, she is unhappy with her house and neighborhood. Several of her friends have moved into nicer homes, and she feels left out. Feeling awful for the past month, it got even worse last week when she learned that yet another friend is moving out. "Now I'm fearing for the future," she said.

She went on to say she has been in her home for thirteen years, and although she admires people who have lived in their homes for 30 years, it's not for her. She regrets feeling this way, but it does not change her feelings. Furthermore, she claims she wants to give to the Lord but has been unable to. What should she do?

The first question to ask is: "Brianna, what would God say for you to do?"

As believers, when we face issues like Brianna's, God wants us to start focusing on Him. He asks us if we have been reading and studying His Word. Has Brianna? Probably not. Brianna needs to realize that God has answers for her in His Word.

What about her church? Does she attend regularly? Does she have friends there she can share her concerns with? Are there any women's groups from which she could receive prayer support? Each of us needs support from friends, especially friends who are Christians. This is part of the reason God established His church—to provide support for us, His adopted children. Hebrews specifically addresses this when it says we are to:

> *Hebrews 10:25 ". . ." not forsake our own assembling together, as is the habit of some, but encouraging one another, and all the more, as you see the day drawing near."*

The second question is: "Brianna, are you honest with Thomas?"

She did not want to burden Thomas with her desire to move.

Brianna needs to decide whether her desire to move stems from her neighborhood changing or from feeling left out and jealous of her friends. She also needs to come to grips with why she has anxiety about the future. Then she can explain her fears to her husband. He needs to know that she avoids being open with him because she fears that he will get upset and leave. But if her fears strain their relationship for very long, the marriage could be in jeopardy. They need to have an open and honest discussion.

Action Steps: Let's also explore other actions, such as how Brianna and Thomas manage their finances. The stress they are experiencing indicates they haven't entrusted their finances to the Lord. One of the wonderful promises of living and managing our finances God's way is a decrease in stress. This

doesn't mean everything will be perfect. There are no guarantees that we won't face the consequences of our actions or decisions, but we can find peace Knowing that God will provide what we need in His timing, Brianna and Thomas need godly counsel on how to manage their finances God's way. Most people, even Christians, do not know these principles. They need to seek it out as a hidden treasure because finding it will be as valuable as one. See the Resource Section for more information.

In the meantime, this coach recommends they begin this process by tracking and categorizing all spending for 30 days. Tracking for 30 days will reveal their current spending patterns. Then, to reach their goal, they must establish a spending plan together.

When Brianna and Thomas are united financially, and as she begins receiving emotional support from her husband, friends, and church, her attitude will improve. Imagine the security this will bring to their marriage. We all need support.

It is easy to be influenced by our neighbors and friends who are moving up the ladder. Just today I saw a 'hot' car parked near mine. Yes, it would be nice to have a newer car, but it is not needed. If the Apostle Paul had to learn to be content, we certainly could learn it as well.

As noted, God wants to give us blessings. It may be that He will give Brianna the blessing of financial freedom. However, she and her husband must first humble themselves before God. recognizing that He is in full control. This means choosing to be content while they patiently wait for Him. Matthew underscores the proper order (His plan):

> *Matthew 6:33 says, "But seek first His kingdom and His righteousness; and all these things shall be added to you."*

Questions to Consider:

1. If you were in Brianna's shoes, what would you do? How would you overcome your fears for the future?
2. Consider the statement: One of the beautiful assurances of managing our lives and finances God's way is a reduction of stress. Do you agree with this? Why or why not?

Chapter 5: The Hard Path to Financial Freedom

If I compare this to learning how to fly, one of the hardest concepts to master was the 'flare' needed for landing. For some reason, I just couldn't send the correct movements from my brain to my hands to perform this important step. To my instructor's frustration, I would actually land without a flare, which was dangerous.

Finally, when he was frustrated enough, he said:

"**Here are the keys, do your solo!**"

When endeavoring to land on my solo, I came in too sharp, and he said he had to **'look away; it was too painful to watch.'** Fortunately, I was at the beginning of the runway and had enough room to reposition the plane, so I could and did land properly! But what a chore!

Life with our finances is like this sometimes as well—a major chore. The next story is about a couple who had to keep trying to make it work.

Life Lesson #20. 'Can The Ends Meet?'

What One Couple Had to Do To Get Their House In Order

Jerry and Laura, both college graduates, were in good health, had good careers, and purchased a house. Then the children came along. Now, if Laura chooses to work outside the home, most of her earnings will go to childcare. Jerry's job cut back on healthcare options and put him on commission.

Trying to cover the expenses of two kids, the house, and two cars on less income was not their plan. It is taking all their funds plus more. Jerry has used most of his retirement savings (and paid the penalty) to help with their costs, and even that has not been enough.

Now he has $20,000 in credit card debt and is moving balances back and forth among cards to keep interest payments low. Their present circumstances make it obvious that they cannot afford their lifestyle. Where is this leading them?

Action Steps: If they continue their present course, this situation will lead to bankruptcy, adversely affecting his employment.

First, they need to examine their expenses carefully. At this point, they can't afford options, only requirements. They *must* cut their costs until they are no greater than their income.

1. Health care: Jerry's job cut his benefits, but there are still other options. It is possible they can split up the health care, with some of the family on his company program and others on another one. Some doctors offer cash discounts for people without insurance or who must pay out of pocket because of high deductibles.

2. They could also join a small group and share problems together.

> Proverbs 15:22 says, *"Without consultation, plans are frustrated, but with many counselors they succeed."*

3. God knows this couple's needs, and He has a plan to assist them. They need to find His plan.

4. Employment: Laura has a college education. Depending on her skills, she needs to pursue a part-time job that she can do at home. It would be great if it had health care benefits.

5. Children's clothing: Good clothing can be purchased at used clothing centers. Friends, ideally from their church, could work together to share items as needed, including swapping outgrown clothes.

6. Repairs: Jerry could consider doing the needed work on their home. If he is not a handyman, he may be able to swap services with others in his church who are. Maybe they can do a plumbing job for him, and he can paint a room in their house. The point is that the body of Christ is made for situations like this. But it takes effort, humility, and prayer.

7. Entertainment: Cable TV needs to go. It is typically a luxury and, in tight times, an easy expense to eliminate. What about cell phones? Do they have expensive plans? How can they be minimized?

8. Food: As with most people, Jerry likes to eat out at restaurants. But cooking and eating at home typically costs one-third of what it costs to eat out. For now, there is no money for eating out, including lunches. Unless there is a business meeting, Jerry needs to bring his lunch.

9. Automobiles: Both have recent cars. Could one be sold? Can they get by with one car? For example, could Jerry work from home one day a week? If so, Laura could use Jerry's car for grocery shopping and other necessities – perhaps even doctor's appointments – on that day. If working from home

is not an option for Jerry, could he ride share or pay for a ride to work one or more days a week? The cost of paying for an extra car, maintaining it, insuring it, and eventually replacing it is high. If exercising this option worked for them, it would save them thousands of dollars each year.

10. Other automobile considerations: Where are they taking their cars for repair? I advise against taking a car anywhere for repairs without having a recommendation or two from those knowledgeable in this area.

The Big Car Repair: Years ago, my wife and I had a popular van that made a loud clunk every time she shifted gears, especially when going from drive to reverse or back again. She took it to the nearby dealership we routinely used for service.

"You need a new transmission," they said. "That'll be about $2500" (typical price then).

I did not feel at peace about that. Sometime earlier, my father-in-law had recommended a transmission company on the far west side of town. My wife made an appointment and limped the car there for confirmation. She watched while they put the van on the rack and worked on it. After a short time, they came to her with the results.

"You've got a bent "dog bone strut," the mechanic said. "That'll set you back about $250, give or take."

A little while later, she drove away with a clunk-free van that ran perfectly. The total bill? $241, including a transmission fluid change—**less than 10 percent of what the dealer would have charged! Thank you, father-in-law.**

Does this mean you should never take your vehicle to a dealer? No, but it does mean you should **obtain counsel** before taking it *anywhere* for service.

> *Proverbs 12:15, "The way of a fool is right in his own eyes, but a wise man is he who listens to counsel."*

We frequently ask other Christians we know and respect for recommendations on car repair businesses. We now have three companies we use. One is a privately owned tire company that does much more than tires. When one of our vehicles needs maintenance, we take it there first. The people know us, give us great advice, and we recommend them to others.

If they cannot do what is needed (and they will tell us), we go to an "official" auto repair company. They can do anything. However, if the transmission is a problem, we take it to a transmission shop recommended by the tire company. We have had great results with these three companies for almost 20 years.

What did Jerry and Laura do in response?

Step One: Laura found a good-paying job that she could do a few days a week from home, during which time her neighbor watches the kids.

Step Two: Jerry and Laura began holding "financial meetings" together, which put them on the same page and gave them greater wisdom (see Proverbs 12:15, above). In addition, this communication strengthens their marriage as they go through these tough times. As a result of their meetings, they decided to keep Jerry and the kids on his health insurance and cover Laura through a Christian healthcare company. In their situation, it was significantly less expensive for just Jerry and the kids to be on his insurance rather than have family coverage.

Step Three: After a few months, Jerry and Laura realized their changes were a start but not enough. They still had credit card balances of $20,000 and other unmet obligations. They revisited their options. First, they could sell their home. After checking with a real estate broker, they realized their house had greatly appreciated. They could net more than the $20,000 needed to pay off the credit cards. But then where would they live?

Step Four: After praying more, Laura asked her family if they could move in with them for a few months to save money. They agreed. Jerry and Laura sold their home, paid off credit cards and other debts, and moved into her parents' house for what turned out to be nine months. During that time, they saved all the money they could and, with a reasonable down payment, bought another home farther outside the city.

With careful spending, they are now on the plus side. **Not only are they saving money each month, but since their credit cards are paid off, the money saved goes back into their long-term 401 (k) retirement account**.

However, the most significant change they made was to begin holding regular "financial meetings." This enabled Laura to be in the know so she could offer her worthy insight.

I have found the solutions my wife produces, on occasion, to be amazing. Solutions that never would have occurred to me. I have heard other guys express the same. Because Laura was in the know, she came up with the idea of living with her parents. The proceeds from the sale of their current home, plus nine months without housing expenses, provided the opportunity to get back on their feet. Now they have a new start.

"There were many tough decisions, but all were worth it in the end," Laura observed. **They DID make the ends meet**. "Praise the Lord."

One option they discussed but decided not to pursue was selling Laura's car. After carefully considering their financial situation, they decided they could afford both vehicles. However, according to Laura, it was a tough decision.

"The money they could have saved," she said, "would have been nice, but if they are able to afford it – a situation always subject to change – it will be more convenient having two vehicles."

Today's world is changing. A second vehicle is nice, but with Uber, Lyft, and other services, it is typically not the requirement it once was.

Questions to Consider:

1. What changes would you have made if you were Jerry and Laura?_____
2. What do you think about "financial meetings"? Did this assist them in discovering God's plan for them? _____
3. Would financial meetings assist you in discovering God's plan for you? If so, who would you ask to have those meetings with?_____
4. Would the one-car option work for your family?_____

Life Lesson #21. What NOT to do. Alisia and the diminished value of her home.

Real estate is one of this country's most common and successful avenues for building wealth. **Many people have purchased a home with a small down payment, paid it off in 20+ years, and realized tremendous gains with two-to-four percent inflation each year**. We want to discuss how to do this, but first, we need to know that it does not always work out that way. Ask Alisia.

In 2006, just before the Great Recession, Alisia purchased a home near a major interstate on the west side of a large city. At the time of purchase, she obtained two loans totaling $275,000. **Note: She has already made two mistakes. First**, she purchased it too close to a major interstate. **Second**, because financing standards were more relaxed at that time and appraisals were as well, the banks looked at her good credit and loaded her up with two big loans in an overpriced home, **with NO down payment!**

In 2018, with interest rates much lower, she endeavored to refinance the house, but it appraised for only $90,000! **A house in the $275,000 range in 2006 is worth only $90,000 in 2018! Is this possible?** Yes! This is an extreme example, but neighborhoods and other factors change, including mortgage parameters.

In 2006, mortgage guidelines were much more 'relaxed,' meaning easier to meet. This led to practices like low-documentation loans, where a bank could approve a mortgage based solely on the applicant's statements, with little or no verification. These practices were easily abused and resulted in people acquiring homes they were not qualified for. It also caused homes to sell for prices higher than realistic. What probably happened to Alisia was a mix of neighborhood change and relaxed mortgage rules, leading to this severe devaluation.

Action Steps: First, if Alisia continues making her house payments (so she is in 'good standing' with the company that gave her a loan) and speaks with the lending institutions involved, it is reasonable to expect they might write off a portion of her loan. After all, in this case, the banks and their appraisers were part of the problem. Now they can be part of the payment solution. However, at least a large part of the problem will remain. Unless a miracle happens, Alisia could lose considerable money when she eventually sells the house. This could have a substantial negative impact on her finances over her lifetime.

The point is that if we do things wrong, purchasing a home might not be a good investment. The example above shows what happens when neighborhoods, mortgage parameters, and interest rates change.

So how do we do things correctly?

1. **Purchase what you need, not what you want. Then focus on paying it off as fast as possible**. Alisa purchased a big house for only her and one child, so she was making a 'statement.' Second, **she put no money down, so she had a relatively big house payment**—which was/is difficult to deal with.

2. **Analyze your 'spending plan.**' How can you spend less and save more? Before you think about purchasing a house, you need a substantial down payment. This may or may not be your problem, but it can be a barrier difficult to overcome. You may want to discuss this issue in a one-on-one Zoom meeting.

3. **Save as much as possible before the purchase** so that your down payment will help you qualify for the 'best deal' mortgage. Note: Routinely, the demand for mortgages fluctuates, and there are sometimes better 'deals' than others. For example: In 2024, if you have good credit—which would be a credit score of 720 or greater—with a 10% down payment, your **interest rate would be approximately 6.2%, plus the following**: Since you have less than a 20% down payment you will have the obligation of Private Mortgage Insurance, which can cost in the range of **$150 or more per month**.

4. **But if you save enough so that your down payment is 20% or more, then you achieve two things**: a lower interest rate, but even more, **you lose the obligation to have Private Mortgage Insurance (i.e., the $150/month noted above).** As noted, the mortgage climate fluctuates. Contact your real estate professional and/or mortgage banker for current parameters.
5. **Once you have purchased, focus on paying off your mortgage early.** I know that it will be difficult to focus on paying extra on your mortgage when you just purchased this house, and there are MANY things you want to do to it, but it is important. For example, **the Reference Section (page 153) has an example of an 'amortization schedule.' It shows the secret of how you can save thousands of dollars of interest on your mortgage and pay it off early at the same time.**
6. **Another idea is to obtain a 15-year mortgage.** This will require a higher monthly mortgage payment, but as noted above, you will literally save yourself thousands of dollars over the life of the loan.
7. **The best idea might be to ask the mortgage personnel what the 15-year payment would be.** If you can, you pay the 15-year payment (and when you do, your mortgage should be paid off in 15 years). But occasionally, if you have

an emergency and cannot make the 15-year payment, you can switch to the 30-year schedule without penalty, which is what I did on one of my houses.

Note: It was interesting to me when I began paying extra on my mortgage, the bank personnel sent me a note saying that I overpaid my payment, and so I would owe less on the next payment. I responded that the extra was to go toward paying down the principal. She did not understand that concept. To help her understand, I began sending in two checks each month. One was for my regular payment and one for the extra principal—with a note in big letters—EXTRA PRINCIPAL. She finally understood!

Questions to Consider:

1. How can we avoid making the mistake Alisia made? What would God's plan for her have been? Remember, she had two loans totaling the purchase price. Do you think she should have sought outside/godly counsel?
2. What cautions would you suggest in purchasing a home?

3. **Do you think it is wise to purchase a home now?** I would probably answer the question by saying: It is always a good time to save money. The more money you have saved, the more options you will have. First, you will find it easier to obtain a mortgage. Second, the lower your house payment will be. Third, this will allow you to seek wise counsel about whether now is a good time to purchase a home.

> *Proverbs 15:22 "without consultation, plans are frustrated, but with many counselors they succeed."*

Life Lesson #22. Maria Kennedy—now a widow

Maria Kennedy's husband, Hank, died of a heart attack 21 months ago. He had always been the financial one in the family, paying all the bills and carefully managing all the accounts. As a result, their house was paid off, and they had a substantial savings account.

As is often the case, this heart attack came without warning. It was a traumatic event for Hank's wife, and she was in a state of shock for months afterward.

"After he died," she told her coach, "I just avoided looking at the finances. I paid the bills, including some of my adult daughter's expenses, and just watched as the savings account balance decreased."

Twenty-one months later, she realized that something had to be done. She had only $3,000 left in the savings account, and the taxes on her home were due next month. "The taxes will take most of what's left," she said.

"If I don't do something different, I will soon be out of money and probably out of my house. What should I do?"

Her social security and other income do not match her expenses. Every month she has had to either dip into her savings or borrow on her credit cards. With almost nothing left in savings, she owes $2,800 on the cards. Fortunately, she has full equity in her home, but to borrow from her home would create another bill to pay, continuing her spiral downhill. And with her savings gone, additional expenses will cause her to borrow even more on her cards.

Her coach made two recommendations. "First, discontinue paying any of your adult daughter's expenses." It is possible she may not have been open with her daughter about her dwindling account, especially if there had been no problem before her husband died. But because there is a problem now, she needs to admit it and allow her daughter to accept responsibility for her own finances.

"Second, you need to get some sort of a job," the coach said. "If you need training or have an emergency, you could borrow on the equity in your home, but you shouldn't do it for any other reason. With decent employment, you should be able to pay back a training loan and provide for yourself."

Maria agreed with the coach's suggestions and said she had recently spoken with an organization interested in hiring her. To satisfy their requirements, she would need to complete some training, which would take several months, but the salary for this position was substantial (for her), so it would justify borrowing on her home equity to support her during this training period.

When she starts this job, she can pay off her credit card and other bills and start saving for her retirement. With her home paid for, she should save enough to satisfactorily fund her retirement, both through her company and independently.

Questions to Consider:

1. Hank was wise to pay off his house and build up a significant savings account to reduce his

wife's stress. What else could he have done to support her during this difficult time?

2. One ministry, **Compass—finances God's way (www.compassfinancialministry.org)**, has a study called **"Set Your House In Order."** It contains a workbook for the husband and wife to write down all necessary information in one organized place so the spouse left will at least know whom to call for an attorney, accountant, or investment advisor, as well as the location of accounts, etc. What do you think of this idea?

Life Lesson #23. John Keller – now a widower.

John called to say, "My wife just died. I need advice."

This example demonstrates that trauma in the death of a spouse is not limited to sudden deaths that come without warning, as it had with Maria Kennedy's husband. John's wife had cancer, allowing him to process this significant event over time, but it still left a hole and diminished strength and judgment.

John needed advice about prioritizing obligations. He had funds to work with because of a $170,000 life insurance policy, but he also had debts. In addition to a home mortgage of $135,000 and a car loan of $5000, he wanted to save for his children's college.

The coach suggested that because John is still working, his priority should be establishing an emergency savings account of at least six months of income. In 2018, this would be around $30,000. Second, he should pay off both his mortgage and his car, which would use the remaining $140,000 of the insurance funds. However, with his mortgage and car paid off, he should have a sufficient monthly surplus to add to his college and retirement funds.

Doing this will significantly reduce the pressure on John's monthly obligations and give him great peace of mind. First, he has substantial equity in his house because it is paid for. Second, he has a satisfactory emergency fund; third, his car is paid for. All he needs to do is take care of routine bills and focus on funding his children's higher education and his future retirement. Although tithing was not discussed, we recommend including this in these calculations.

Questions to Consider:

1. Why does John need the $30,000 in savings as an emergency fund? First, how secure is his job? No one knows. Circumstances change, and the days of working for one company an entire lifetime are history. Second, he could have health problems that would cause him to miss work or even lose his job. Third, one or more of

his three children could have health emergencies or other problems. God knows that in this fallen world, we will face emergencies from time to time. This is the reason He gave us the plan.

> Proverbs 21:20 (TLB), which says, "The wise man saves for the future, the foolish man spends whatever he gets."

2. If you were John, would you make changes to these recommendations? What and why?_____

Life Lesson #24. What about life insurance?

James is a professional but not in life insurance. Following a friend's advice decades ago, he bought a term life policy for himself. Now about to retire, he called with a question.

"Should I keep my term life insurance? It was recently renewed, and the cost has gone way up. I do not think I'll be able to make the payment on my retirement income."

"What does your insurance agent say?" the coach asked.

"Well, he has been calling repeatedly. He says I should buy whole life insurance instead, because it's important to have life insurance.' But it is even more expensive."

"Why do you need it?" the coach asked.

"What do you mean?" James said. "My agent says everyone needs it."

"Lots of people do," the coach answered, "but not everyone. The primary purpose of life insurance is to provide for a spouse and children if the breadwinner dies. It can also be used to fund a child's college education or to fund an estate. It may be necessary at one point in your life, but not at another. **The question you need to answer is, what do you envision the insurance money going for? What need will it fill?**"

"I don't know," he said.

The coach said, "If you have no plan for it, if you have no real need for it, then why keep paying for it?"

This was a revelation to James. He and his wife were thankful for the question. The coach encouraged them to pray about it for a few days and perhaps obtain other counsel before making their final decision. They agreed.

Action Step: The agent James spoke to did not have his best interest in mind but was simply trying to sell another policy. It is essential to have a trusted professional looking out for your best interest and providing counsel.

Please note that there is an essential place for life insurance, especially for younger families. If the breadwinner dies, the one left behind (usually the wife) will need funds to support herself and the children and possibly provide for college. <u>Term life insurance costs are reasonable for younger families and highly recommended</u>.

However, for James, this revelation will save him and his wife hundreds of dollars each month and thousands each year. These are dollars that can go directly to long-term investing.

The Scripture that could apply here is in Proverbs.

> *Proverbs 15:22 "without consultation, plans are frustrated, but with many counselors they succeed."*

Questions to Consider:

1. Do you agree with the coach's question, "If you have no plan for life insurance, then why keep it?"_____

2. What about your life insurance? Are you comfortable with your level of life insurance coverage?_____
3. Who would you ask for advice about this?
_____

Life Lesson #25. Kimberly Manwell and a will.

In these two recent stories (Life Lessons 22 and 23), both families had wills. What happens when a parent dies without a will? In this next story, it could have happened.

"My husband and I have two young children," Kimberly wrote to her coach, "but we don't have a will yet. What do you recommend? Should we have it done by an attorney?"

This is a great question; one every young couple should ask. The first part of the answer is, **"Don't wait any longer!"**

The driving force behind this urgency is the important question: Who will have custody of your children if you die before they turn 18? It's best to have legal help, but it's crucial to get it done quickly. One legal firm in the United States found that 69 percent of parents with minor children have NOT chosen guardians. This could lead to a potential disaster.

Action Step: Without a will, a judge might easily assign custody based on factors different from the parents' values. A non-Christian relative who is better off financially could be chosen over someone who is committed to the children's spiritual growth. Even worse, depending on the financial situation or lack of it, the children could end up in foster care. If either of these scenarios occurs, what are the chances they will grow up to be believers? Will they ever see them in heaven?

Another issue that needs careful consideration is asset management. **Without the specific guidance of a will, judges are likely to release all assets to the children when they reach the ripe old age of 18.** Will they be mature enough to manage these assets at this age? For most children, the answer is no, not even close. For a biblical reference to this, see Luke 15:13.

The best recommendation is to use an attorney (ideally one in their church) to draft a will that includes a testamentary trust for the children.

Questions to Consider:

1. Do you have a will? _____
   Is it current, or are there changes in your situation that could affect its ability to enforce your wishes?_____

2. If you personally completed your will, have you considered the implications of a trust or other adjustments to keep your estate out of probate?_____
3. A verse to consider:

> Luke 15:13 says, "And not many days later, the younger son gathered everything together and went on a journey into a distant country, **and there he squandered his estate with loose living.**"

Question: Which of the stories in this chapter do you relate to the most?

_____
_____

What actions are you going to take because of your conclusion?_____

Week 6: Ensuring Long-Term Financial Stability

The Unvarnished Truth

Reading previous chapters, it is hoped that you have bought into the correct manner of managing the money you are responsible for and **have now begun saving a portion of all funds received**.

But your money should not just sit in a savings account, making a paltry amount of interest. Once you have more than three to five thousand dollars, it should be working for you. You say, "How can I make the money work for me?"

Here are five case studies: five individuals who have been successful (in their minds) with their investments over approximately 10 years. Will they be successful in the future? There is no guarantee.

However, they are intelligent, comfortable with their investments, and seem on track to achieve their goals. **The question is, can you apply any of their ideas to your investment plans?**

Note: It is highly recommended that each investor do their own due diligence before initiating any investment.

Life Lesson #26. Growing Dividends: Aaron carefully researched the stock market, consulted the contacts he had, and developed the following investment strategy:

He planned to invest in the stock market, but only in companies with a record of <u>growing dividends</u> over the last 20 years. This also means they never decreased dividends. He wanted/needed good dividends because that is what he and his family would live on in the future, and he also wanted to protect the money (the principal) he was putting into these companies. Therefore, before investing, he carefully researched companies with strong dividend yields. The questions he asked were:

1. How long have they been paying those dividends_____
2. Had they dropped their dividends in tough times?_____
3. How has the stock price done over the years?_____

4. What rating did they have from the rating companies?_____

He concluded that companies with strong answers to these questions are most likely to survive economic downturns. Therefore, that became his focus. Note that reports are available that show much of this information.

Aaron said, "My concern is, what is the dividend, and how sure am I that the company will continue to pay that dividend?" He knew that the broader market would occasionally take the stock down, **but the question is, did the company reduce its dividend during that time?**

What gains did Aaron obtain over his ten years? He estimated he received a total return of better than 220 percent. If we compare this to the S&P's total return over the last ten years, it **is 125 percent if dividends are reinvested**. This shows the benefit of being selective in his stock investment; **since Aaron focused only on the best-paying dividend stocks, he did substantially better**. <u>Note that this is just an estimate</u>.

Life Lesson #27. Corporate Bonds: Robert also wanted income from his investments but was uncomfortable with the stock market. He was always concerned about the downturns. However, he is interested in bonds, especially corporate bonds, because they have higher yields.

Note: A corporate bond is a bond issued by a corporation and is debt it 'takes on' to raise capital for various purposes such as expansion, acquisitions, or operations. Corporate bonds typically have higher yields because they carry a risk of default and no insurance against it. However, if it is properly researched, he felt he could do well there—and, more importantly, he has friends who do well in this arena.

He wants investments that:

1. Provide interest rates at those of current investment-grade corporate bonds.
2. Provide monthly dividend payments (as many stock dividends are)—although that is not always possible.

In the last decade, according to the Internet, "corporate bonds can routinely provide interest rates higher than those available with Certificates of Deposit." However, this type of investment carries less security, and corporations that issue corporate bonds can be stretched too thin and default.

Returns fluctuate greatly, from .22% per month in 2021 to 4.85% per month in 2024. This translates to an annual range of 2.64% in 2021 to 58% in 2024. Such a difference is significant, and the key takeaway is "buyer beware." **If we average these numbers and multiply by 10, the total 10-year return is approximately 290%. Remember, this is only an estimate.**

As Robert would say, if you have the potential for this much return and have done quality research, you can justify some risk.

Life Lesson #28. Certificates of Deposit: Rachel is suspicious of corporate bonds; she is also uncomfortable with the stock market in general. Her parents never had the funds to invest, and she had heard horror stories about people losing money there, so the whole idea made her uneasy. Always concerned about downturns, she chose to keep her money in local banks. She purchases their long-term Certificates of Deposit and likes that the federal government guarantees them up to $250,000. Since she has more than $250,000, she has her Certificates of Deposit in multiple banks.

In the last ten years, Rachel would have made a total return of 40 to 45 percent on her money. She feels safe with this investment and comfortable with this outcome. **Note that this is just an estimate**.

Life Lesson #29. Gold and Silver: Peter is concerned about the economy and the vast U.S. government debt (increasing at a rate of approximately 3 trillion dollars per year). As a result, he has insecurities about all the above, including the value of the U.S. currency. Therefore, he has invested most of his assets in gold and silver bullion and coins. He has stored these in various well-maintained storage facilities outside his home, even some outside the country.

Calculating the price of gold and silver then and now, it is estimated that over the 10-year period from 2016 to 2026, he would have achieved **a total return of about 360 percent.** He said he is blessed at this point, as the metals have had significant increases in their value in 2026. Also, because of the continued increase in U.S. government deficit spending (resulting in the Federal Reserve needing to print more and more money), he feels serious inflation is on the horizon—and, in that case, his precious metals will continue to do well. **Note that this is just his estimate.**

Note also that, through 2025, Peter's 10-year return was significantly less, totaling about 80%. Whether he will retain the 360 percent return remains to be seen.

Life Lesson #30. Various Strategies: James uses a combination of strategies.

1. He has funds that he puts in Certificates of Deposit.
2. He has purchased some dividend stocks.
3. He has also purchased some silver that he keeps at home.
4. He has purchased property outside of the U.S., and a missionary is renting it. He regards it as a possible future residence for him and his wife.
5. He has also bought a large amount of cryptocurrency because he wants funds outside the banking system, and he believes certain cryptocurrencies will perform well in the future if the dollar loses value.

In the last ten years, he estimates his **total return is 100 percent or more**, although he does not know what value to place on the property outside the U.S. He also says his cryptocurrency (which is down now) should go up exponentially in the future—an idea most crypto investors have. **Note that this is just his estimate**.

In conclusion, it's interesting to see the big differences in the returns these investors say they've achieved. The main goal of this exercise is to show that there are many options available—and to give you, the reader, some insight into the choices you can make—so that, with good advisors, you can make the best decisions for yourself and your family.

As we have discussed the Holy Bible many times in this book, it would be appropriate to note some of its points on investing. They are as follows:

- **Seek wisdom from many counselors/advisors (as recommended above). Proverbs 11:14.**
- **Diversify your investments. In other words, do not put all your 'eggs in one basket.' Ecclesiastes 11:2.**
- **Recognize our role as stewards and avoid get-rich-quick schemes (such as gambling or highly leveraged investments). Proverbs 13:11 and Proverbs 28:20.**

Note also that there are investment options other than those presented. It is highly recommended that the reader speak with several professionals (counselors/advisors) of their choosing to determine which options would work best for them.

Chapter 7: A Life That Matters-- Choices and Rewards

Are we just here for a moment and then gone? Are our lives worth anything? Does it matter when we do good or evil? Who knows what we have done? Does it matter what we believe?

What evidence is there to support that anything matters—after all, evolution says, "We just happened." Is that true? What is true?

Take this book, they call the Holy Bible. Is it true? It says God created us, but as one lady said, "<u>Didn't men just write it? How do we know it is correct?</u>"

It bothered me when she said this, but it is a good question. **How do we know the Holy Bible is correct when it says God created us?**

Here are some considerations:

1. **Evolution versus Creation**: All public schools in the United States are required to teach that evolution is true, that it is a proven fact. They base their argument on Charles Darwin's 1859 treatise, which they claim is correct in stating that a single cell is a simple organism easily formed from available chemical components.

    But what real evidence do we have today?

    There is a book, **Answers Book 1: Over 25 Questions on Creation/Evolution,** edited by Ken Ham and written by experts in their fields, that addresses the question: Could evolution, in fact, have happened? In the book, he quotes Dr. Michael Behe, Associate Professor of Biochemistry at Lehigh University, Pennsylvania. Dr. Behe states that, contrary to Darwin's assumptions, the objective evidence shows **"the simplicity that was once expected to be the foundation of life has proven to be a phantom; instead, systems of horrendous irreducible complexity inhabit the cell."** For

further information from Dr. Behe, see his book, Darwin's Black Box.

**I find this quite fascinating. If the single cell is supposed to be the beginning of life, how could each cell contain 'systems of horrendous irreducible complexity'?
Is this not a contradictory statement?
Later, he notes that each tiny 'simple' cell *constantly requires thousands of biochemical reactions* to stay alive and perform its functions.**

According to another biochemist, the thousands of reactions noted above are at least five thousand biochemical reactions, which must be at the same level, in the correct concentrations, and in the absorbable form necessary for the first cell to begin its existence!

The point is, how could this system of 'horrendous irreducible complexity' just happen? Logic says it could not have happened; it would be impossible. Therefore, it <u>had to be created</u> by somebody or some 'superpower.' So, who was/is that 'superpower'

Let's look at the evidence of a 'superpower.'

2. **Multiple eyewitnesses—Rising from the dead? The big question in the Holy Bible is whether the Messiah, Jesus of Nazareth, rose from the dead. What proof do we have of this event? If He did rise from the dead, He is of divine origin. However, His disciples initially did not believe He had risen. They did not think He was alive. After all, they had watched Him be crucified, die, and buried. As a result, they were so afraid for their own lives that they hid in a locked room!**

    But suddenly, they changed completely! They became fearless and traveled all over the known world, telling everyone that He had died and risen again. Not only that, but all of them, except one, were martyred for their faith—because they kept saying Jesus was alive and that He had risen from the dead!

    Question: Why would these men die for something if it was not true? The answer is, they would not. Therefore, they really did see Jesus alive.

    Three days ago, He was dead. But because they personally saw and touched Him, and Thomas even put his hand into His side, they now knew He was alive and was the Son of

God He said He was. And everything else He said was true as well. What a transforming event!

Powerful? Yes, incredibly so!

The point is that, based on the historical facts of His disciples' transformation and many other things from the Holy Bible, we can confidently say that God did raise Jesus from the dead and, therefore, can do anything He wants to do, such as creating us.

He can also inspire His chosen prophets and disciples to write an accurate Holy Bible with the same rationale. <u>So, men did not just write the Bible; they wrote it after seeing the risen Jesus and wrote only what He inspired them to write</u>.

3. **Fulfilled Prophesy**: In any history books, do you know, or can you find evidence of a country losing its borders, and losing all its people, and ever coming back again? Think about it and see if you can find anywhere that there ever was such a country.

    I ask this question because there has never been such a country.

Throughout all of human history, spanning thousands of years, there has NEVER been a country that lost its borders and its people and then regained its sovereignty. EVER.

Except for one. Not only did it happen once to that country, but it happened twice! What a fantastic thing, right?

What is the country? Israel. But why did it happen? It happened because the people of Israel kept disobeying God.

He warned them repeatedly, but they refused to listen. So, he did what he said he would do.

What does this indicate? It once again affirms that there is a true God. It demonstrates that He was active in their lives and, therefore, can be active in ours as well. Furthermore, He has the power to do whatever He desires. What an idea! The good news is that this is just one more piece of evidence that He is real.

 If you want to read some of His prophecies about the reformation of Israel, check out in the Holy Bible, Jeremiah 30, Isaiah 66:8, and Ezekiel chapters 37 and 38.

It all comes down to the point: **God is real, and He has the power to create this world and us. Because we**

are here, He exercised that power. Therefore, if He talks about something, we should listen, right?

In reality, we should listen to everything He says, but now, **let's talk about how we can have a relationship with Him.**

Many Bible verses teach these truths; among them are:

> *Romans 10:9-10 ". . if you confess with your mouth Jesus as Lord, and believe in your heart that God raised Him from the dead, you shall be saved; for with the heart man believes, resulting in righteousness, and with the mouth he confesses, resulting in salvation."*

This Word from God says, if you pray a sincere prayer like the one above and invite Jesus, the Christ, the Son of God, into your heart as your Lord and Savior, when you die, you will go to heaven and be with Him for all eternity.

If you have invited Him into your heart, the question now might be—what's next? What's next is your opportunity to live with a Savior who loves you and desires the best for you. He has a plan for your life. His plan is to help you develop the talents He has given you to not only support yourself but to advance His kingdom in some form. This will give you a life filled with meaning and the blessings of inner, supernatural peace. As the Apostle Paul says in Philippians:

> **Philippians 4:6-9 6 Be anxious for nothing, but in everything by prayer and supplication with thanksgiving let your requests be made known to God. 7 And the peace of God, which surpasses all [a]comprehension, will guard your hearts and your minds in Christ Jesus.**
>
> **8 Finally, brethren, whatever is true, whatever is honorable, whatever is right, whatever is pure, whatever is [b]lovely, whatever is of good repute, if there is any excellence and if anything worthy of praise, [c]dwell on these things. 9 The things you have learned and received and heard and seen in me, practice these things, and the God of peace will be with you.**

The above statement has a lot to it. This is the reason churches exist: to help us understand what it means to live for Him and to support us as we endeavor to carry out the process.

The obvious next step is to find a good church, attend it, and participate in it. If it is a good church, you will find fellowship, friends, godly instruction, and blessings.

If the reader wishes to discuss this further, please feel free to e-mail me at luke1611@pm.me.

Additional Note: Evolution is widely accepted but can be easily disproven. If you're still unsure whether there is a real God who created this world and want more information, I invite you to read one or both of these books: "The Case For Christ" by Lee Strobel or "Answers Book 1" by Ken Ham.

Another topic discussed in the Holy Bible is tithing.

Tithing is giving a certain percentage of your funds to further His Kingdom. My wife and I personally participate in this activity, and I believe that because of this, God has worked in us and in the lives of our family in powerful ways. This is the reason the 10/10/80 division of your funds is recommended in this book.

Three uplifting stories discuss tithing 10 percent. I share these with you for your consideration.

Life Lesson #31. What happened when Nathan gave his tithe?

My good friend Nathan related this story. More than twenty years ago, as a growing Christian, Nathan decided to get serious about Christianity. This included humbling himself to the Almighty God in every way. He felt called to begin reading his Bible regularly and to begin tithing, giving ten percent of his gross personal income to his church. He had a stable job, which he liked, but after tithing, there wasn't much surplus cash.

Nathan and his wife wanted children, but none were forthcoming, and testing confirmed their inability to conceive. They prayed about it, and at his suggestion, they decided to pursue adoption.

Nathan felt like God was leading him to adopt a little boy, which his wife wanted as well. They felt blessed when, a short time later, they found an orphaned little boy who was available for adoption.

But there was a problem. A large fee was required at the time of adoption, much more than Nathan and his wife had. In his prayer to God, he prayed: "God, you gave me this desire to adopt a little boy, and you have put us in contact with one we could adopt. But you know what our finances are, and our inability to pay the adoption fee. Will you help us?"

Shortly thereafter, an 80-year-old lady called Nathan at his work. She said she did not trust banks, and she had a large sum of money stored at her house. She said she wanted to meet Nathan and possibly have him invest it for her.

Nathan met her at her house. After meeting and speaking with him, she decided she could trust him.

"I want you to take this cash to your office and invest it."

"No," he said, "I can't do that, but if you will meet me at the bank, we can invest it just like you want."

She met him at the bank and gave the money, all $48,373, to the teller. Nathan told me he would remember the exact amount of this money for the rest of his life. The teller then provided Nathan with a cashier's check from the lady made out to his company. Nathan took the check and invested it as the lady had requested.

The commission Nathan received from the investment was exactly the amount he needed to complete his little boy's adoption. God has a soft heart for orphans and amazing ways of answering our prayers.

A Scripture applicable is:

> *James 1:27 (NIV), "Religion that God our Father accepts as pure and faultless is this: to look after orphans and widows in their distress and to keep oneself from being polluted by the world."*

Life Lesson #32. What happened when Emily trusted Him by giving?

This story comes from one of our female coaches. Sometimes we meet someone and can just tell they have their act together. That's how it was when I met Emily. She was a manager at a well-known company in her town, and when I was introduced to her, she said she was interested in joining our team as a financial coach. Emily quickly completed the training and coached women for several years, doing an excellent job.

One day, while meeting with a lady seeking counsel, she shared a story. She said that years ago, she went through a difficult divorce, which her husband wanted, and life was hard for her. As a single mom with a small child, she struggled to make ends meet. Her finances were very tight, and her deadbeat ex-husband was little help. His child support was, at best, sporadic.

Her church at the time made a plea for a special gift. When she prayed about it, she felt God asking her to make a substantial gift. She told God this was her grocery money until the next pay period, two weeks away, but she gave it anyway.

With tears in her eyes, she said that a few days later, she received a check in the mail from her deadbeat ex-husband for over $2,000, which was considerably more than she had given to the church. The envelope was dated the same day she had given the money. God works in powerful ways in our finances – and in the rest of our lives.

But He requires us to trust Him first.

The Scripture applicable here and in the next lesson is in Malachi:

> *Malachi 3:10, "Bring the whole tithe into the storehouse, so that there may be food in My house, and test Me now in this," says the Lord of hosts, "if I will not open for you the windows of heaven, and pour out for you a blessing until it overflows."*

Life Lesson #33. What happened when Jasmine and Mike obeyed Him by giving?

Jasmine told this story in her small group. She said she and her husband, Mike, were just making it financially. They were Christians and really trying to follow God's plan for their lives. Several times, they had talked about tithing, but they just did not see how they could make it happen financially.

In an effort to start tithing, they began working overtime at their jobs. Yet when they worked overtime, they were so tired afterward that they lacked the energy to prepare supper at home. So, they ended up stopping at fast-food restaurants to eat before arriving home.

Jasmine said to her husband, "This is ridiculous. We are trying to earn more, and we are spending every bit of it on eating at restaurants. We are not getting anywhere."

After praying about it, they decided to take the plunge and begin tithing.

Jasmine said, "It was exactly 14 days later that she received a raise in pay at work. And it was not just a raise. It was a big raise."

We may never know for sure on this side of heaven, but it seems that almost immediately after Jasmine and Mike started tithing, her supervisor submitted her request for a pay increase. It took two weeks to take effect, but the process was started right after they obeyed.

Jasmine and Mike's hearts were right. They desired to obey God, so they stepped out in faith and were blessed for it.

Questions to Consider:

1. What do you think of the tithing examples presented? Have you, or someone you know, had an example of God working in this manner?
2. Has God ever worked in your life the way He worked in the lives of these people?
3. Do you think God could work in your life the way He has worked in the lives of the last three examples? Why or why not?

MAJOR POINTS

Most of the major points in this book are summarized in these 12 brief paragraphs, each of which contrasts a common secular opinion with what God says in Scripture. My prayer is that these points will mean as much to you as they have to me. I also believe these points summarize His plan, His proven plan, guaranteed to help us on our earthly journey.

1. **The world says,** "All the stuff you own is yours. Your name is on the title of your car, so it is yours." **But God says,** *"The earth is the Lord's, and all it contains, the world, and those who dwell in it"* (Psalm 24:1). Our Lord says He made it in Genesis 1. In Psalms and other places, He says He owns it, not you, not me.

2. **The world says,** "Since it is all yours, manage it your way." **But our Lord says,** *"Moreover, it is required of stewards that one be found trustworthy"* (1 Corinthians 4:2). What is a steward? A person who manages something for someone else. Since we are stewards of what our Lord has given us, we need to be trustworthy and manage all "our" assets His way.

3. **The world says,** "Go ahead, buy it if you want it. Debt is no problem as long as you make the

payments." **But our Lord says,** *"Just as the rich rule the poor, so the borrower is servant to the lender"* (Proverbs 22:7, NLT). The Lord says He wants us to be a servant to Him, not to the lender. The Lord also says in 2 Kings 4:1-7 that debt is dangerous. **And when we are in servanthood to the world, we have stress. Our Lord wants to minimize our stress.**

4. **The world says,** "Stand up, be your own man or woman, and make your own decisions." **But our Lord says,** *"The way of a fool is right in his own eyes, but a wise man is he who listens to counsel"* (Proverbs 12:15). Our Lord knows how easy it is to be swayed, so He says to seek godly counsel before we make major decisions. This way, we are less likely to make the decisions the world wants us to make and more likely to make the ones He wants us to make.

5. **The world says,** "It does not matter if you need to stretch the truth; just say whatever you need to say to get whatever you can get." **But our Lord says,** *"You shall not steal, nor deal falsely, nor lie to one another"* (Leviticus 19:11). Our Lord commands us to be honest.

6. **The world says,** "Gimme, gimme, I want more, more, more." **But our Lord says,** *"It is more blessed to give than to receive"* (Acts 20:35). The Lord knows that "more, more, more" will not make us happy. Instead, His focus on living and giving will make us happy.

7. **The world says,** "Do as little work as you can get by with, and be paid as much as you can get for it." **But our Lord says,** *"Whatever you do, do your work heartily, as for the Lord rather than for men . . . it is the Lord Christ whom you serve"* (Colossians 3:23-24). He says that we are not working for our boss sitting in the next office; we are working for the Lord God in heaven. We need to do our best all day long. Howard Dayton tells the story about the carpenter. "Just as the carpenter builds the house, so the house builds the carpenter. It refines his skills, teaches him patience and perseverance. He is a better person after he built the house than before." We need to realize that work was made for our benefit, that it helps us grow to become the person He wants us to be.

8. **The world says,** "Invest to get rich, the quicker, the better." **But our Lord says,** *"Steady plodding brings prosperity; hasty speculation brings poverty"*

(Proverbs 21:5 TLB). To be happy and have less stress, *we* need to follow His recommendation.

9. **The world says,** "You have a life to enjoy. Put those 'rug rats' into daycare, pre-school, kindergarten, and year-round public school." **But our Lord says,** *"These words, which I am commanding you today, shall be on your heart. You shall teach them diligently to your sons and shall talk of them when you sit in your house and when you walk by the way and when you lie down and when you rise up"* (Deuteronomy 6:6-7). Passing our faith to our children is a key responsibility. Fulfillment in life includes making it a high priority.

10. **The world says,** "The person who dies with the most toys wins." **But our Lord says,** *"For I have learned to be content in whatever circumstances I am. I know how to get along with humble means, and I also know how to live in prosperity"* (Philippians 4:11-12). True happiness includes being contented. Our Lord wants us to get our priorities correct. Trust Him with all things. He will provide for us. *"But seek first His kingdom and His righteousness, and all these things shall be added to you"* (Matthew 6:33).

11. **The world says,** "You only go around once in life; grab for all the gusto you can get." **But our Lord says,** *"For what shall it profit a man to gain the whole world and forfeit his soul?"* (Mark 8:36). This world is but a preparation for eternal life to come. This is our proving ground, our preparation for when we will be with our Heavenly Father for all eternity--when we have accepted Him as our Lord and Savior. It is to our benefit that we give Him our all now, while we can, and do work that will last for all eternity.

12. **The world says,** "Enjoy life; spend your money; have fun with it." **But our Lord says,** *"Therefore if you have not been faithful in the use of unrighteous [worldly] wealth, who will entrust the true riches to you?"* (Luke 16:11). True riches are a close relationship with our Lord, something we can enjoy both now and for all eternity. Will we be faithful in the use of our worldly wealth? Will we hear our Lord say the words in Matthew 25:21 to you? *"Well done, good and faithful [servant]. You were faithful with a few things, I will put you in charge of many things; enter into the joy of your master."* This is our goal. This is our plan. This is ending well.

Resource Section.

1. Companies that assist with credit card difficulties

This government-sponsored site lists many reputable companies that provide this service.

https://www.consumer.ftc.gov/articles/0153-choosing-credit-counselor.

The following are firms with which this author has had contact. No remuneration is received from any firm noted, and no guarantee is provided or implied.

a. Credit.org: www.credit.org/cccs. 800-431-8157

b. National Foundation for Credit Counseling: www.nfcc.org. 800-388-2227

c. **Trinity Debt Management: www.trinitycredit.org.** 800-758-3844

2. Debt Snowball Method.

How to pay off Credit Cards faster. If you are in credit card debt and want to pay your cards off faster, here is an excellent method: the "**debt snowball method.**"

Here is how you do it: List the credit cards in order of balance, with the largest first. List the card, the balance, the interest rate, and the minimum payment, as shown in the following example.

Bank of America	$12,583	28%	$232
Citibank	$9,832	30%	$148
Wells Fargo	$2,945	30%	$46
Chase	$1,212	28%	$35

1. We *always* pay at least the minimum amount shown on every card, and we must always pay it *before* the due date. A late payment may raise the interest rate even higher.
2. Choosing the card with the smallest balance, in this case, the Chase card, we pay the minimum plus as much extra as we can each month. Let's say we're tight on money, but we can scrape together an additional $50 to pay toward the Chase card. We pay $50 plus $35, for a total of $85 on the Chase card. If we do this every month, it will pay off the card much faster.
3. After Chase is paid off, we take the $85 we were paying on Chase and add it to our minimum payment on the next-lowest card (Wells Fargo). Adding $85 to $46 means we are now paying $131 on the Wells Fargo card. If we do this every month, it will pay this card off much faster as well.

This assumes we can scrape together only an extra $50 per month to pay on the cards. If we can pay more, the debt is paid off more quickly. It also assumes we don't put any additional charges on the cards that we can't pay off at the end of each month. For example, if we have a card that we typically use for gasoline, we continue to use it, but we always pay all the current gasoline charges along with our monthly payment. We ensure we do not add extra charges to the card unless we can pay them off at the end of the month.

The benefit of using this method is that we will become debt-free more quickly.

Jasmine came to one of this author's classes because she had serious credit card debt. When the debt snowball system was explained to her, she went home and calculated how long it would take if she used this system on her credit cards versus what she was already doing, which included adding extra to the smallest card she was focusing on first.

She came back the next week, excited to say, "**The debt snowball method paid my cards off over one-third faster!**"

Note this included adding extra to the smallest card, the one she focused on first. After that was paid off, she continued to add the extra to the next smallest card, as noted above.

This results in substantial savings for us. Do the card suppliers tell us this? No, they want us to take as long as possible to pay off the cards. This is the reason they suggest the minimum payment option in the first place!

3. National Consumer Credit Reporting Agencies

To the author's knowledge, there are three national consumer credit reporting agencies in the United States. Their names, addresses, telephone numbers, and website addresses are shown below.

Equifax. P.O. Box 740241, Atlanta, Georgia 30374. Telephone: 888-766-0008. www.equifax.com.

Experian. P.O. Box 9554, Allen, Texas. 75013 Telephone: 888-397-3742. www.experian.com.

TransUnion. P.O. Box 2000, Chester, Texas 19016. Telephone: 800-680-7289. www.transunion.com.

For further information regarding these companies, please contact the Bureau of Consumer Financial Protection, 1700 G. Street NW, Washington, D.C. 20552.

4. How to Place a Freeze on Your Credit

Because of security leaks, many (including this author) have chosen to **freeze their credit.** This does not freeze the credit they currently have with their mortgage, credit cards, etc. **It prevents any new credit (from a thief, for example) from being added until the freeze is removed or lifted temporarily. Note: At this time, there is NO charge for initiating or maintaining the freeze.**

To put a freeze on your credit, send a note to all three credit reporting agencies at the following addresses: Equifax Security Freeze, P.O. Box 105788, Atlanta, Georgia 30348 (telephone 888-298-0045); to Experian Security Freeze, P.O.

Box 9554, Allen, TX 75013 (telephone 888-397-3742); and to TransUnion, P.O. Box 6790, Fullerton, CA 92834 (telephone 888-909-8872).

In your note, request a freeze to prevent any new credit from being added to your account. Include your complete name, address, social security number, and date of birth. They will respond with confirmation of the freeze and a password to lift it, either temporarily or permanently, as you direct.

This password allows you and only you to lift the freeze. If you desire to add to your credit (for example, if you are changing your cell phone from one company to another).

Caution: Please be aware that there are no guarantees of anything in this life, including the success of a credit freeze. As demonstrated by major security breaches at credit companies, no system is perfect.

5. How to Obtain Your Credit Score

If you wish to obtain your credit score, write to one of the companies noted above and provide your social security number, your full name, address, and date of birth. Enclose a self-addressed, stamped envelope. Or contact them online at their website.

6. How to Avoid Paying Interest on your Credit Cards

Credit card interest rates vary: as of now, some rates are 30 percent annually – without late-payment penalties. If

we borrow money on our card, the rate can be 34 percent or higher. If we're late on payments, the rates can increase significantly.

How do you pay zero interest? Pay it off in full--*before* the due date, every month!

7. Envelope System For Budgeting

The envelope system for budgeting is basic, but sometimes it is the best. Here is how it works. Use an envelope for each spending category. For example, use one envelope for *home/apartment expenses,* such as rent and utilities. Another for *clothing,* another for *car expenses,* including car payments and maintenance. Another for *food/groceries,* another for *eating out,* another for *miscellaneous,* and so on. Make certain there is one for *saving* and one for *tithing* as well.

Take your paychecks to the bank and cash them so you have all this money in cash. Then, divide the money into the required categories listed above, allocating the necessary amounts to high-priority expenses first, such as home/apartment rent, utilities, and car payments.

After covering your high-priority payments, decide how to allocate any leftover funds among optional categories like dining out, clothing, or entertainment. For example, once you've paid the essential bills, you might have $80 set aside in the envelope for dining out this month. This means you should limit your dining-out spending to that $80 for the month. When the money in that envelope is gone, you can't spend more in that category until next month.

The purpose of this plan is to clearly show us how much money we have in each category and to limit our spending to the predetermined amounts. **If you have difficulty controlling your spending, this is an excellent plan.** I first heard about this from Larry Burkett, and I have heard about it from other ministries and programs since because this plan works.

Note: If you do not want to convert everything to cash but you like the idea of the envelope system, I recommend taking a piece of paper, writing the total net income you receive each month (or each pay period) at the top, and listing your categories below. If you are married or together, decide how much should go in each category. Make certain the totals of all the categories do not exceed the total of your (net) income.

Next, prepare sheets of paper for each category, with the category name at the top. Then, each time you spend Money, you write down the amount spent on that paper. category. Again, the total for the category cannot exceed the total amount agreed for that category.

If you do this consistently, it will work out the same as the cash envelope system. However, the envelope system is more visual and makes it easier to see when you are out of money in a particular category.

8. Form for Monthly Income and Expenditures

1. Total (Gross) Salary/Income_____
2. Tithe _____
3. Savings_____
4. Income Tax Estimated_____
5. House Mortgage/Rent_____
6. Housing Insurance and Taxes_____
7. Housing Utilities_____
8. Other Housing Costs (maintenance)_____
9. Food (Not Eating Out)_____
10. Auto/Truck Payment_____
11. Fuel_____
12. Auto Insurance_____
13. Auto Expenses (maintenance)_____
14. Insurance (medical, etc.) _____
15. Entertainment/Recreation/Eating out_____
16. Clothing_____
17. Medical_____
18. Miscellaneous_____
19. School/Childcare_____
20. Investments/Retirement_____
21. Debts/Credit Cards/Loans_____

Total all expenses _____

Income minus expenses equal surplus_____

Note: Actual spending plans may have many more categories. Feel free to make copies and alter this.

Amortization Schedule

(How to save money by paying less interest)

Let's talk about how to pay your house off early. The next page shows an amortization schedule, which itemizes the interest and principal paid each month.

If you have a $275,000 mortgage at an interest rate of 6.0%, amortized over 30 years, your payment schedule for year one is shown in the chart on the next page.

If you choose to pay your normal payment in month #1, it is $1,375 in interest + $273.76 in principal, for a total payment of $1,648.76. **However, note the high-lighted $275.13 in month #2 below—this is the principal on your loan for the next month. If in month #1 you choose to pay your normal payment of $1648.76 + $275.13 (the principal for month #2), then you jump to month #3 for the next payment, and you never have to pay the $1373.63 of interest due for month #2! You just saved yourself a whopping $1373.63**. This is a substantial savings! Do the banks tell you this? No, they want your money, but this is the way it is.

If you do this every month, your loan time will be cut in half. Note that as you pay down the loan, the interest part of the payment will decrease, and the principal will increase. But the premise remains.

Amortization Schedule:

	Beginning Balance	Interest	Principal	Ending Balance
1	$275,000.00	**$1,375.00**	**$273.76**	$274,726.24
2	$274,726.24	$1,373.63	**$275.13**	$274,451.10
3	$274,451.10	$1,372.26	$276.51	$274,174.59
4	$274,174.59	$1,370.87	$277.89	$273,896.70
5	$273,896.70	$1,369.48	$279.28	$273,617.42
6	$273,617.42	$1,368.09	$280.68	$273,336.75
7	$273,336.75	$1,366.68	$282.08	$273,054.67
8	$273,054.67	$1,365.27	$283.49	$272,771.18
9	$272,771.18	$1,363.86	$284.91	$272,486.27
10	$272,486.27	$1,362.43	$286.33	$272,199.94
11	$272,199.94	$1,361.00	$287.76	$271,912.17
12	$271,912.17	$1,359.56	$289.20	$271,622.97

Year #1 End

The above schedule is for a $275,000 mortgage at 6.0% for 30 years, meaning that if you pay the agreed $1,648.76 payment (the total of interest and principal) every month for 30 years, it will be paid in full. However, as noted, if in month one you pay $275.13 in addition to the $1648.76, you avoid ever having to pay the $1373.63 interest for month #2. If you are confused about this, take it to your local banker for further explanation.

9. **There are many good companies that teach 'finances God's way.' The two companies below are those this author recommends.**

Compass—finances God's way.
Website: www.compassfinancialministry.org.

Vision: To see everyone, everywhere, faithfully living by God's financial principles in every area of their lives. Mission: Equipping people worldwide to faithfully apply God's financial principles so they may know Christ more intimately, be free to serve Him, and help fund the Great Commission.

Ron Blue Institute
Website: www.ronblueinstitute.com.

The Ron Blue Institute (R.B.I.) exists to communicate and integrate biblical financial wisdom into schools, churches, companies, and communities, transforming how people talk, think, and behave with money. For more information about the resources available through RBI to help transform your community, visit the website noted above.

Index

Week 1: 'Breaking Up With Broke.'

Life Lesson #1. Marcie and the high-interest car loan.

Life Lesson #2. When one spouse does not do their part.

Life Lesson #3. Judith's son asked her to refinance her home.

Life Lesson #4. Pastor Leon, and his new blue pickup truck.

Life Lesson #5. Ken and his hot muscle car.

Life Lesson #6. Let's talk about credit.

Week 2: Taming Your Financial Excesses.

Life Lesson #7. What 'success' can look like.

Life Lesson #8. Louann and her medical bills.

Life Lesson #9. Marty, afraid to tell her husband.

Life Lesson #10. Donald and his consolidation loan request.

Week 3: Need vs Want: The Ultimate Showdown.

Life Lesson #11. How to deal with co-signing.

Life Lesson #11b. How to avoid co-signing.

Life Lesson #12. Johnny Bedford the construction worker.

Life Lesson #13. Janice and her $9,000 credit card debt.

Life Lesson #14. What to do with an arrogant husband.

Life Lesson #15. Gladys and her adult children.

Life Lesson #16. Gloria asked what to do about her son.

Week 4: This Is Not Working!

Life Lesson #17. Jerome's concern about his wife's spending.

Life Lesson #18. A test in Adam and Jenny's marriage.

Life Lesson #19. Brianna has no peace.

Week 5: Hard Path to Financial Freedom

Life Lesson #20. Can the Ends Meet?

Life Lesson #21. Alisia and the diminished value of her home.

Life Lesson #22. Maria Kennedy, now a widow.

Life Lesson #23. John Keller, now a widower.

Life Lesson #24. What to do about life insurance.

Life Lesson #25. Kimberly and her will.

Week 6: Ensuring Long-Term Financial Stability—The Unvarnished Truth

Life Lesson #26. Growing Dividends.

Life Lesson #27. Corporate Bonds.

Life Lesson #28. Certificates of Deposit.

Life Lesson #29. Gold and Silver.

Life Lesson #30. Various Strategies.

Week 7: A Life That Matters--Choices and Rewards

Life Lesson #31. What happened when Nathan gave his tithe?

Life Lesson #32. What happened when Emily trusted Him by giving?

Life Lesson #33. What happened when Jasmine and Mike obeyed Him by giving?

ACKNOWLEDGMENTS

There are many to thank for creating this book. First and foremost, my wonderful wife, who provided valuable insight from the beginning. It was her idea to begin each chapter with an airplane story, as she lived through most of them.

As is true for many of us, our mothers have spoken into our lives. My mother provided continual encouragement and guidance. I am thankful for my father, who felt called to ministry in his college days, and never wavered from his faith in the Almighty God or in his calling to preach.

In the 'finances God's way' ministry I am most thankful for Howard Dayton. His many books have left an indelible imprint on my heart and mind. Because of his ministry, I was introduced to my great friend Hank Kulhanek. Hank's continued guidance and encouragement have been critical to this book. Also helpful was Howard Dayton's editor, Steve Gardner.

I am also indebted to my good friend and lifelong attorney, Steven Hall, as well as Pastor Dave Altman, Denny Fulk, Bob Eldridge, Gary Bolenbaugh, and Derek Wallace. Derek was the foremost in the continual support I received in ministry. Then there are guys who prayed for me regularly, Gary Martin and Jim Wisler. In addition, my cousin Scott Toussaint has been a continual encouragement and partner in ministry for over a decade.

I also received valuable advice from authors I met at homeschool conventions. If you have never attended one, you have missed out. I owe Janet Smith a thank you for our yearly activity there. Additionally, her husband Wes, an author himself, provided important insight.

Finally, I am thankful for those represented in this book. Their trials, triumphs, failures, and successes have been incorporated with other stories to create what you have read here.

My prayer for everyone involved is to receive many rewards, now and eternally, for what you are doing for the kingdom.

About the Author

After graduating from Asbury University, David taught high school chemistry, served honorably in the US Army, and pursued various careers until God took a firm hold on his life. Since then, he has been teaching 'finances God's way' in North, Central, and South America. He has led over 60 classes and coached hundreds of participants. He now shares many of his engaging stories in this book.

David has also authored the original "**When Money Gets Personal,**" "**Keep The Change,**" for teens/young adults, "**My Friend Patches**" for ages 5 to 10, **GIVE SAVE SPEND GOD'S WAY** for ages 4-7, and **Problemas En Las Finanzas? Aun Hay Esperanza!**" for Spanish-speaking audiences. All are available on Amazon.com/books. He is supported by a wonderful wife, children, and grandchildren. For further information, or to contact the author, please visit www.whenmoneygetspersonal.com

www.ingramcontent.com/pod-product-compliance
Lightning Source LLC
Chambersburg PA
CBHW050748100426
42744CB00012BA/1937